AND
FINI
SHE
S

FOR
INTE
RIOR
S

MAT ERIA LWO RLD

INNOVATIVE STRUCTURES AND FINISHES FOR INTERIORS

BIRKHÄUSER — PUBLISHERS FOR ARCHITECTURE
BASEL • BOSTON • BERLIN

FRAME PUBLISHERS
AMSTERDAM

PRE FAC E

THE GREAT DISAPPEAR-ING ACT

ED VAN HINTE

It's extremely light, incredibly strong and soundproof. It looks and acts exactly as you want it to, performing automatically and even disappearing when not needed. It's the ideal material, a substance that technologists and designers have been searching for throughout the ages. The reality, however, is something altogether different. Because there you are, after two hours in the lift, having reached the three-hundredth floor of a skyscraper groaning from the agony of self-repair. Moving through an automatic door that dawdles as it opens, you enter a dimly lit room that's a bit on the chilly side, and the choice of piped-in music doesn't help matters either. The chair you select is uncomfortably warm, though the table has a nice design – too bad the scent of freesias is so overpowering. The transparent floor lets you gaze down at the atrium 50 metres below, a great view if you're not scared of heights. The cup on the table is edible, but at the moment it contains 'a fluid that is almost but not quite entirely unlike coffee'. Scenario and citation come from *The Hitchhiker's Guide to the Galaxy*, Douglas Adams's old but unsurpassably witty sci-fi classic, which mocks human weaknesses and the peculiarities of science.

Technological development is one of the latter. It takes place on the cutting edge of a blade whose opposite sides pit the temptation of vast potential against the scepticism implied in the question: Is this really what we want? We invent all kinds of new things to make life more pleasant, but seem to be only moderately successful in achieving our aim.
Material World is a shopping list of new materials, complete with potential applications. The point of such uses is not always evident, but mentioning them is crucial. After all, a material without context is no more than a boring toy. At the very least, you should have an idea of what you want to do with it. Quite regularly I'm asked to spew out a number of typical sustainable materials. My reply is invariably no. Styrofoam can be sustainable, and so can lead and rosewood. It all depends on how you use them. The same applies to properties like rigidity and thermal insulation. A great example of the inextricable ties linking material and application is an LPG tank made of plastic reinforced with natural fibres, a recent project of the Laboratory for Lightweight Constructions, a facility of the Department of Air and Space Technology at Delft University of Technology. Authorities initially rejected the tank, citing the inflammability of the material. Subsequent tests proved, however, that a tank made of this plastic was actually safer than a metal tank, because the former didn't explode when thrown, filled with gas, into a fire. It simply burned up. Within the foreseeable

A MATERIAL WITHOUT CONTEXT IS NO MORE THAN A BORING TOY

future, these tanks will have taken over the market now dominated by their metal predecessors.

The development of materials has a rather split personality, a character resembling that of their creators. We find experts in the field of materials that become immersed in the possibilities of a substance. An example is the guy who works for years analysing the hardness or heat resistance of a technical polymer, even though nobody else gives a hoot.
Occasionally, these specialists discover weird and wonderful phenomena crying out for application in what often turns out to be a desert.
Running parallel to scientific studies are products developed by designers and technicians who discover a need for a material with certain properties and can't find anything that satisfies the requirements. Ezio Manzini's book, *The Material of Invention*, addresses this subject. Better communication

between the worlds of research and application is certainly not superfluous.

Of course, technology continues to make serious strides forward, in spite of its human character one might say. In recent years, the most rapidly advancing area has seen a marked increase in materials whose properties are adaptable to one degree or another. Sometimes this adaptability raises the question of whether or not they can still be labelled as materials. Composites, generally described as combinations of very strong or hard components and a binder – think of reinforced concrete or carbon-fibre-reinforced resins – are, strictly speaking, not materials but constructions. This is because many of the properties involved, from rigidity to soundproofing, are an intrinsic part of the planned arrangement of the components. In the case of variable rigidity, for example, the construction adapts to changing circumstances. Such variability relies on elastic tailoring, which is, by definition, a matter of putting things together.

The bond between material and application works best when it stems from a 'higher' functional necessity; in other words, when the basic story makes good sense and the material plays a subordinate role. The story or line of reasoning can relate to dry technical functionality, but it can also embrace other aspects of an application, such as aesthetics and perception. 'It simply has to look right,' says English architect Richard Horden, referring to the relationship between function and beauty. One of Horden's designs is a 150-metre-high mast in Glasgow with an aerodynamic cross section. The tower turns with the wind, thus saving 30 per cent in superstructure costs. The engineers that analysed the design for Horden had their doubts at first, but after making the necessary calculations, they decided it would work. That was the conclusion Horden had expected to hear, 'because it looked right'.

Stories that don't make sense often emerge from applications conceived for exotic materials with interesting properties whose purposes are not always evident. *Material World* offers examples of such materials, along with descriptions of their extraordinary, almost magical, characteristics. The reader's inevitable response is: We should be able to something with this. Memory metal is one of these highly seductive materials. You can take a preformed object and bend it out of shape, but when it's exposed to a certain temperature (which depends on the composition of the alloy), it automatically reverts to its original form. Somebody used memory metal to make a wind-up teaspoon that subsequently unwinds in the cup, automatically stirring the contents. And years ago a futuristic American architect came up with the idea that construction could be facilitated by heating folded components made of memory metal at the building site. He found it a practical solution, but I doubt that the idea actually produces better results than, say, shaping and welding. This fascination with memory metal also surfaced about ten years ago in the 'New Materials' competitions organised by the Dutch Foundation of Industrial Design. Such attempts rarely produce anything more than a gadget or curiosity, however. An unexciting application like the automatic valve in a ventilation system that opens when the temperature gets too high makes good sense. But incorporating memory metal into sleeves that roll up automatically is not high on the list of anyone's priorities; nor does it offer an aesthetic benefit that isn't simpler or cheaper to realise with existing weaving techniques.

Memory metal occupies the dangerous territory of 'interesting effects', a category well represented in this book. Think of colour, for instance. Visual effects are exciting at first glance, but when unrelated to other functions or occurrences, they inevitably become tiresome examples of kitsch. Thermochromic ink, which changes colour as the temperature changes, is fun to play with, but if the conversion has nothing more to say, the game is over. Effect for the sake of effect stops at the showcase.

There has to be something more to it. That doesn't mean we should write off every material that seems to be stuck in the 'interesting effects' category. The essence of the property behind the effect might still be of use, even if only for something as trivial as an air valve.

Perusing the survey provided by *Material World*, the reader has no trouble deducing the general direction of technological development. What practically jumps off the page is our continual search for stuff that works by itself. Materials that leave us plenty of time to do other things – things that we want to be equally time-saving. We can't read an ad or see a commercial without being reminded of how important it is for products to do the job for us. It would be interesting to make an estimate of when 'by itself' succeeds and when it doesn't. A smart material that reacts to change by repairing itself, by absorbing fluid or by changing shape probably works well if its function remains in the background, divorced from personal taste or intent. Otherwise, the system seems headed for failure. It's very annoying when technology misjudges human behaviour. Watch Jacques Tati's movie, *Mon Oncle*. Or let Muzak frazzle your nerves. Light that switches on and off automatically can be highly irritating if the new ambience doesn't coincide with your intentions. And I wonder how much fun it is to have the decoration of a room respond to your presence but not to your mood.

Another facet of today's technological development is what I like to call 'The Great Disappearing Act'. The aim is to make constructions stronger, lighter and more compact, and to integrate functions into materials. A good question is: Just how much are we willing to accept? Audio equipment is already being integrated into textiles, and according to a recent newspaper article, a Danish team has managed to implant a sort of loudspeaker into a molar. This could portend the disappearance of the mobile phone as we know it. Do we really want to be techno-telepaths?

Or will the urge to display our lifestyle by flaunting the latest model continue to prevail? All this leads directly to the observation of a third trend, which lay dormant while industry claimed centre stage, only to emerge with renewed strength during the last ten years: personification or, as marketing people call it, 'mass individualisation'. Manufacturing methods originally used solely for rapid prototyping – the super-fast fabrication of models – are gradually becoming cheap enough for a type of series production that turns out a diverse range of items. The form of each product is defined exclusively by software, and a computer program is infinitely easier and faster to change than a mould.

BETTER COMMUNICATION BETWEEN THE WORLDS OF RESEARCH AND APPLICATION IS CERTAINLY NOT SUPERFLUOUS

It's an exceptionally fascinating development, because what will determine these individual variations? Theoretically, every consumer can create his or her own products. I don't anticipate a large-scale application of this idea, however. Customers will find it much easier to leave the task up to someone else – a designer, for instance. A good possibility is that flexible manufacturing methods like this one will give rise to a new profession.

Developments in new materials and manufacturing methods are moving in numerous directions. Hybrids now in the making are diminishing the importance of traditional classifications like wood, ceramics, metal and plastic. Mechanical is becoming electronic, electronic is merging into the chemistry of materials, tangible is vanishing into thin air, and action is taking a back seat to the passive experience.

Material World is brimming with illustrative examples, all of which target readers and their projects, and all of which have the potential to spark original ideas. Thanks to relevant addresses, phone numbers, websites and such, the reader who wants more information can go straight to the source. An almost certain result is a new generation of innovative products and materials.

Ed van Hinte (1951) studied industrial design at Delft University of Technology. After a brief partnership in a small design studio, he became a freelance journalist in the area of industrial design. He worked as a moderator for Droog Design in the Dry-Tech project and published several books, including *Lightness: The Inevitable Renaissance of Minimum Energy Structures.* Currently on the editing staff of 010 Publishers in Rotterdam, Van Hinte also teaches design at both the Arnhem Institute of Architecture and the Design Academy in Eindhoven, where he is associated with the master's programme.

SMA
RTT
ECH
NOL
OGY

CONTENTS

NOW
AST
E

CONTENTS

OPT
ICAL
EFF
ECT
S

CONTENTS

FLE XIBL EST RUC TUR ES

CONTENTS

SOU
NDC
ONT
ROL

CONTENTS

STR
ONG
BUIL
DING

CONTENTS

FRE
EFO
RM

CONTENTS

FINI SHIN GTO UCH

CONTENTS

SMA
RTT
ECH
NOL
OGY

INTRO

Intelligent materials are dynamic. They move from one phase to another and back again. In practice, even under changing circumstances (fluctuations in temperature, for example) a smart material remembers and is able to reassume its original form. Many smart materials experience the same sort of life cycle. They are developed for a highly specific application, perhaps for use in the aerospace industry. Later they are discovered and used as gimmicks by manufacturers or designers operating in a totally different field. The final step is further development, which often leads to new applications of a functional nature. Nitinol – a shape memory alloy of nickel and titanium – was used by the United States Navy as a sound-absorbing material in submarines and battleships in the 1960s. It was Japanese industry in particular that launched further research into shape memory alloys in the eighties. One application was to equip coffee makers and electric kettles with automatic switches that shut off when the water boils.

A new generation of fabrics manages heat regulation and fluid balance in the human body. Phase change materials can be incorporated into sportswear to create a product that draws in surrounding heat, stores the surplus energy, and releases it when physical activity ceases or the ambient temperature falls. More static but just as smart are conductive textiles used to make flat, foldable, washable keyboards. The result is ultra-portable electronic equipment that can be integrated into clothing or furnishings.

A completely different category of smart materials includes thermochromic and photochromic pigments, inks and coatings. When exposed to heat or UV light, respectively, they undergo a predetermined change of colour. The seat of a chair with a thermochromic coating changes colour at the point of contact, as if by magic, when the user sits down; a table reacts to a cup of hot coffee in the same way. The world is still waiting for a functional application, however. Of more consequence are Chinese experiments with a smart building paint; thermochromic pigments added to this paint react to outdoor temperatures by changing colour. Applying the coating can increase the temperature indoors by about 4°C in winter and decrease it by about 8°C in summer, making the material a form of passive climate control. Such experiments are the forerunners of buildings that will be equipped with all-round intelligence systems. Such a structure will adapt to its environment by changing colour and temperature, heal itself when damaged, and independently clean its façade and windows.

The speed at which this futuristic image becomes reality depends on the enthusiasm of property developers, architects and end users.

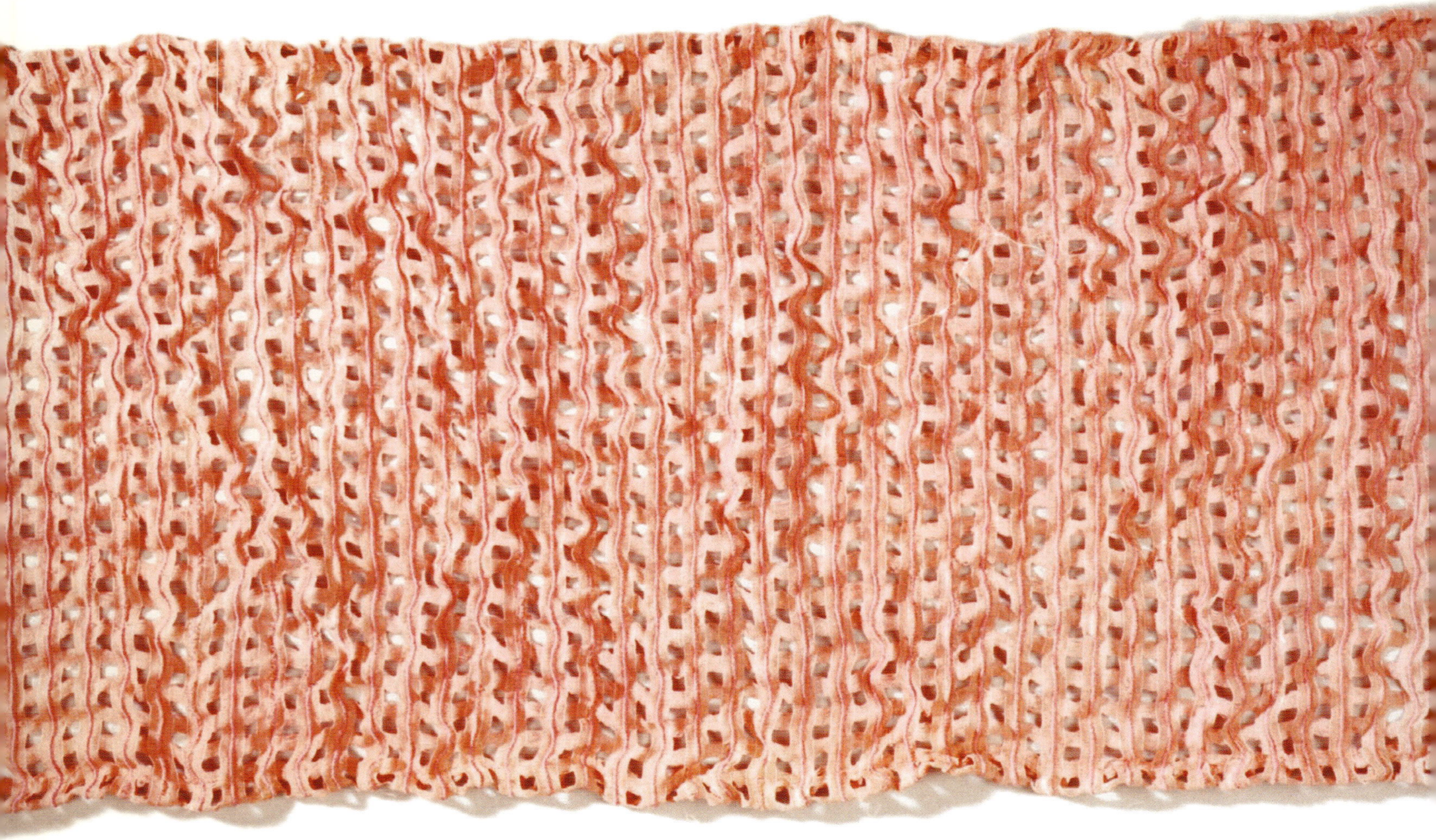

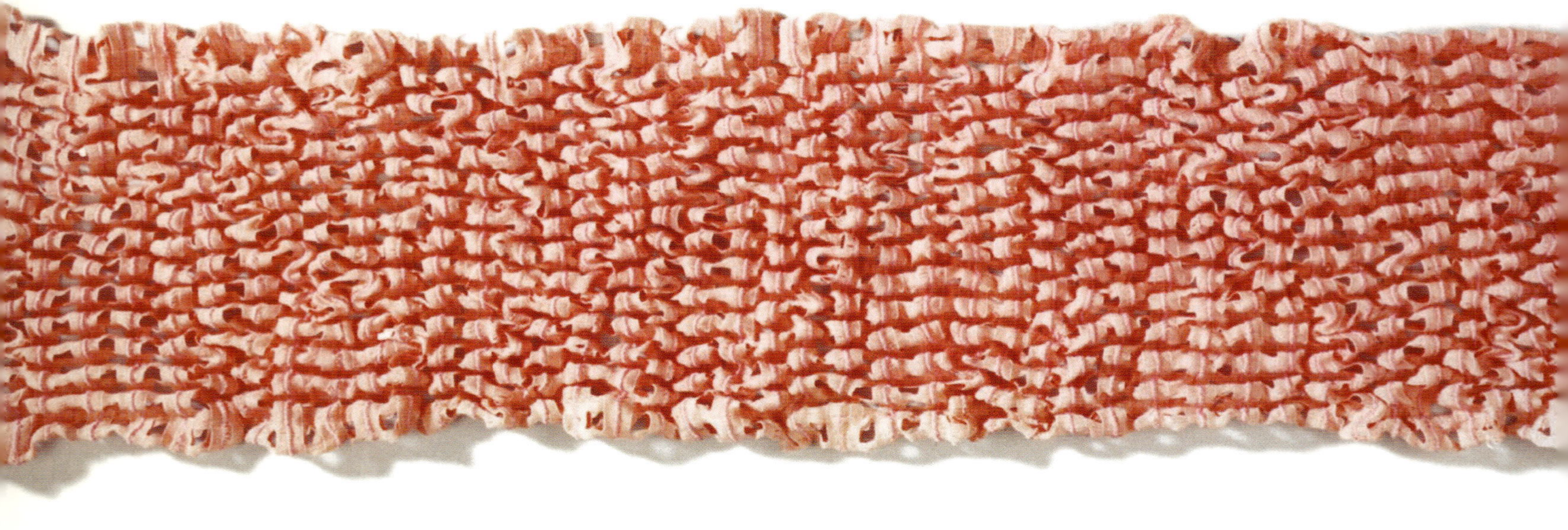

01

TEXTILES WITH SHAPE MEMORY ALLOYS

Composition
Textile, NiTi alloy

Properties
Variable in form, flexible, lightweight, easy to process

Applications
Garments, curtains, sun blinds/screens, blankets, duvets, lampshades

Contact
Mariëlle Leenders
Lavendelplein 2
NL-5643 DD Eindhoven
The Netherlands
T +31 (0)40 848 2890
M +31 (0)6 4185 3055
marielle_leenders@yahoo.com

Photo
Designer Mariëlle Leenders (Design Academy Eindhoven) has experimented with fabric that features shape memory wire either woven into the material or added later as one or more lines of stitching. Her Moving Textiles react to differences in temperature by shrinking, creasing, changing structure or rolling up. Lines of stitching added to the basic material in certain places cause the fabric to creep up when temperatures rise.

Fabrics incorporating wire containing shape memory alloys (SMA) vary in form according to changes in temperature. The thin wire is made of an alloy based on nickel and titanium. This metallic material belongs to a group of related substances referred to as shape memory alloys (SMA). They possess the ability to return to some previously defined shape or size when subjected to the appropriate thermal procedure. Generally, the materials can be plastically deformed at some relatively low temperature, after which – upon exposure to some higher temperature – they revert to their original shapes. The temperature at which the material changes in form can be programmed precisely at any desired temperature between -50° and +100°C. Materials that exhibit shape memory only upon heating have a one-way shape memory. Materials with a two-way memory react to the warmer temperature by changing shape and, subsequently, to the cooler temperature by assuming their initial form. A shape memory alloy deformed at a temperature slightly above its transformation temperature has a high degree of elasticity.
When a similar heating process is applied to Moving Textiles, a material that features shape memory wire, the fabric reacts to later changes in temperature (of more than 2.5°C) by shrinking, creasing, changing structure or rolling up. Normal fluctuations in body temperature, therefore, cause no reaction. But clothing made of Moving Textiles can be programmed to respond to the transition from wintry outdoor temperatures to heated indoor spaces. Examples are sleeves that automatically roll up and down, a jacket that opens and closes on its own, and a shirt that expands and contracts in both length and circumference. Other possibilities are blinds that descend when exposed to warm sunlight and roll back up when the temperature drops. Moving Textiles can be used for both decorative and functional purposes. The material is not yet on the market.

02

FLEXIBLE WOOD

Composition
Compressed natural wood

Properties
Flexible, directly applicable, short production time, chemical free, little material wastage in production, storable in a sealed container (to avoid drying) up to six months if kept cold (below 4°C but above freezing) to prevent mould and fungal attack

Applications
Furniture, yacht interiors and mast rings, signage, exhibition stands, models, timber floor beading, handles, curtain poles, walking sticks, toys, veneers, laminations (Flexywood)

Contact
Mallinson
Unit 5 Gore Cross Business Park
Bridport Dorset DT6 3UX
UK
T +44 (0)1308 427 915
F +44 (0)1308 427 942
info@bendywood.com
www.bendywood.com

Photo
As long as it's wet, Bendywood can be shaped by hand.

The product known as Bendywood is composed of natural wood that has been longitudinally compressed using a patented technique. The resulting material can be bent quite easily at room temperature and set to shape when dried. As a steamer is not used, the bending process is not limited in terms of time. The chemical-free process has the added environmental benefit of reducing material wastage in production. Compared with traditional steam bending, Bendywood can be bent to a tighter radius, and components can be split, parted or twisted. As a result, three-dimensional forms can now be created with greater ease. Even more flexible, Bendywood Extra is used mainly for prototyping. However, once dry it has less resistance to unbending and less stiffness for any given thickness or species of wood. The most commonly used wood is European beech. Limited sizes of other temperate hardwoods (oak, ash, elm, cherry, walnut and maple) can be supplied on long lead times initially. Bendywood is supplied sealed to prevent drying out and setting.
Flexywood, an even more recent development, is permanently flexible until glued or held to shape, but does have a memory. As with ordinary wood, it can be sawed into thin strips and used as a laminate for purposes such as lippings, skirtings and curved countertop edges. Flexywood is supplied kiln dried.

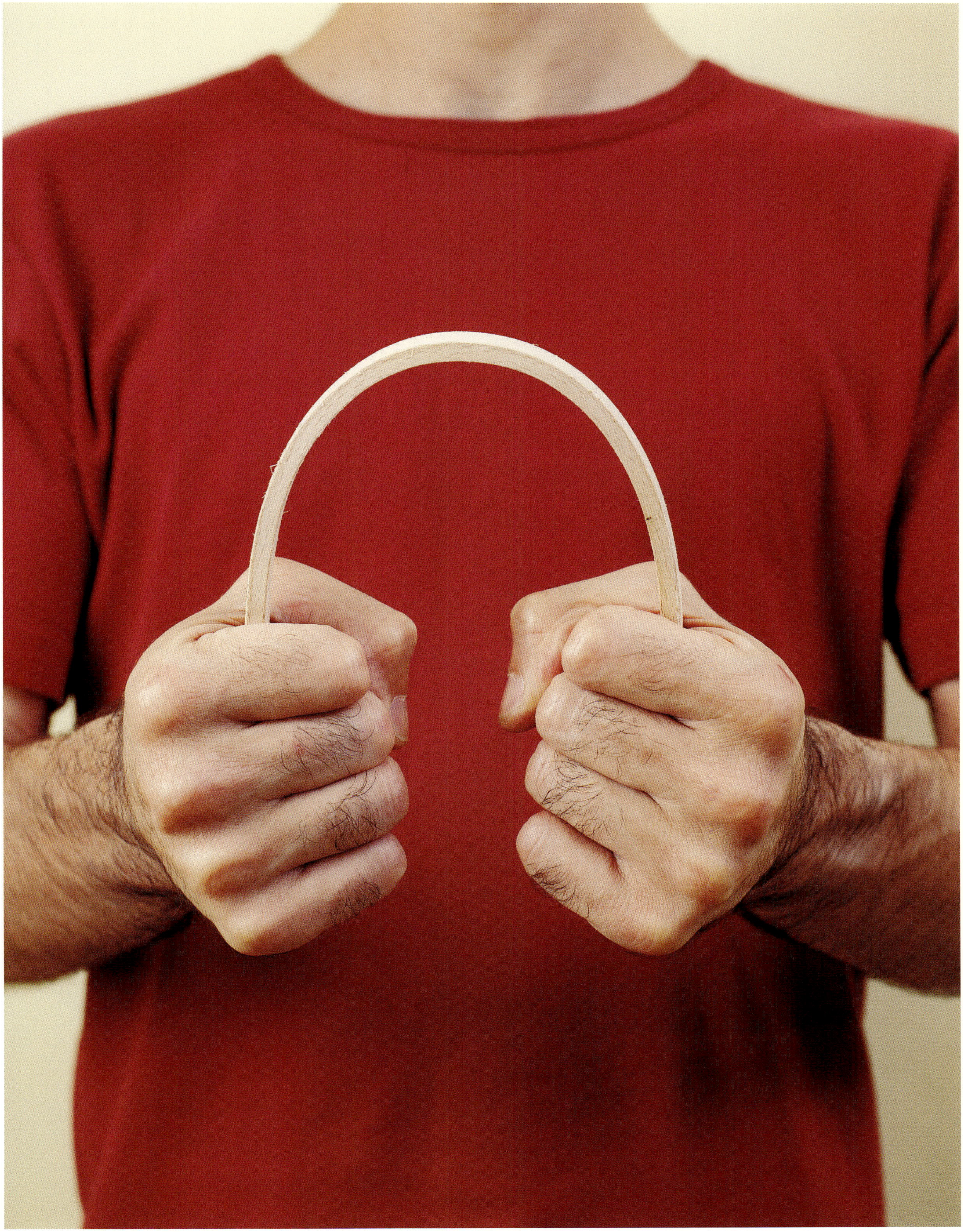

03

THERMO-CHROMIC PIGMENTS

Composition
Printing ink (base ink to which thermochromic pigments have been added)

Properties
Changes colour (for a virtually unlimited period of time), adapts to various temperatures, decorative, functional, printable

Applications
Printing materials, gifts, indicators, prevention of counterfeiting, advertising

Contact
The Pilot Ink
1F Shizuta Building,
3-7-1 Kotobuki, Taito-Ku
Tokyo
Japan
F +81 (0)3 3844 3052
kawagoe@pilotink.co.jp

Flask
Japan
naama@green.ocn.ne.jp

Photo
Japanese design team Flask uses paint with thermochromatic pigments as an experimental finish for furniture. The paint changes colour at temperatures of 36°C or above. Whatever part of a user's body touches the chair, for example, leaves a visible mark on the surface. The phenomenon vanishes several minutes after the source of heat is removed.

The Pilot Ink calls its thermochromatic product Metamo Colour, which is a smart paint that changes colour at temperatures between -20° and +60°C. The ink changes colour in a process that repeats itself almost indefinitely. An entire rainbow of colours is available, and the product can change from colour to colour or even from colour to colourless.
There are three main types: cold (reacts to cold liquids or air, for example), warm (reacts to body heat, warm breath and the like) and hot (reacts to hot liquids, hot air and other sources of heat).
Metamo Colour can be applied to various printing materials and is suitable for many manufacturing processes. It can be used on packaging materials such as OPP, CPP, PS, PET (shrinkage presents no problem), NY and paper. Other materials compatible with the product are synthetic paper, nonwoven fabric, textile, ceramics and glassware. The ink is ideal for cans and bottles containing liquids with a recommended serving temperature. As soon as the drinks are cold enough, the ink or illustration changes colour; in other cases, a message appears on the container. Additional applications are entry tickets and verification seals for the prevention of counterfeiting.

04

PHOTO-CHROMIC DYES

Composition
UV-sensitive pigments

Properties
Changes colour when exposed to ultraviolet light, not highly flammable, various colours available

Applications
Glass, inks, plastics

Contact
James Robinson
PO Box B3
Hillhouse Lane
Huddersfield HD1 6BU
UK
T +44 (0)1484 320 318
F +44 (0)1484 320 300
uk.sales@james-robinson.ltd.uk
www.james-robinson.ltd.uk

Photo
The lenses of these glasses react to UV light by turning colour.
Transparent chips containing photo-chromic dyes react to UV light with a display of bright colour.

Photochromic dyes – one example is Reversacol – are sensitive to UV light, including the ultraviolet rays of the sun. Applied to a wide range of products, these dyes are used for their special chromatic qualities.
The products involved are colourless unless exposed to a sufficient amount of UV light, which changes them into brightly coloured objects. Take the source of light away, and the colour leaves as well. UV radiation breaks a bond in the photo-chromic molecule, which then twists and opens into a planar coloured form; ambient heat causes the material to revert to its colourless state.
The number of colours is virtually limitless, but standard shades are red, purple, blue and yellow. Ironically, the very thing that limits the life span of photochromics is exposure to sun-light, which eventually causes them to fade.
When photochromic pigments are used in plastics, the photochromic effect relies heavily on the physical and chemical properties of the desired polymer matrix. The best properties to look for are a low flexural modulus, higher polymer purity and lower glass transition temperature. Polyolefins, vinyls and rubbers produce a good photochromic response.
A relatively unknown application, still in the developmental stage, is the use of this pigment for photochromic windows. It's an interesting idea, but not an energy-saving solution.
Although photochromic windows successfully reduce sun glare, they are not a good method of indoor climate control. This is because the amount of light that strikes a window does not necessarily correspond to the amount of solar heat the surface absorbs. In the winter, when the position of the sun is relatively low, sunbeams hit the window at an angle of incidence that darkens the glass even more than the UV rays of sum-mer do – and this during the season when homes and offices welcome every bit of solar heat available.

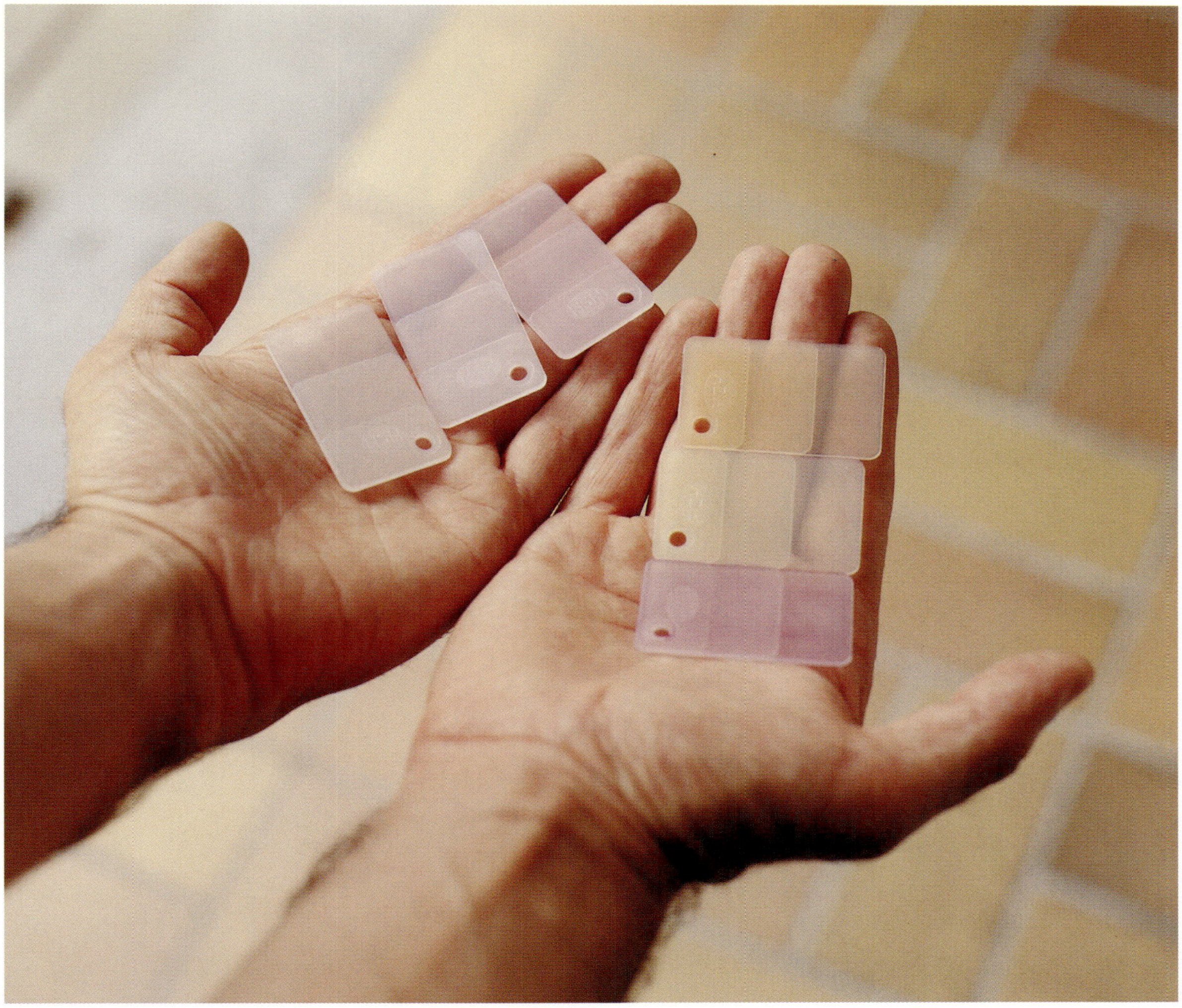

05

ANTI-MICROBIAL FIBRE

Composition
Textile fibres with a coating of 15 per cent silver

Properties
Antimicrobial, antistatic, anti-odour, therapeutic, nonallergenic, chemical-free, transfers heat

Applications
Athletic and outdoor apparel and footwear, medical and hospitality markets, defence and high-tech industries

Contact
Noble Fiber Technologies
421 South State Street
Clarks Summit PA 18411
USA
T/F +1 570 348 2760
info@noblefiber.com
www.noblefiber.com
info@x-static.com
www.x-static.com

Photo
Silver-coated fibres provide garments with natural anti-odour, antistatic and thermodynamic properties.

Known as X-Static, the silver-coated textile fibre developed by Noble Fiber Technologies provides products with natural anti-odour, antistatic and thermodynamic properties. The multi-functional fibre can be used in woven and nonwoven knits and fabrics as a filament or spun yarn. X-Static lasts for the life of the product, because the silver coating is irreversibly bound to the surface. It neither washes nor wears off. The coating process produces a fibre that looks and feels like the fibres used in traditional fabrics. The fibre is a safe and effective antimicrobial solution for garments and footwear. By binding with ammonia, the material eliminates virtually all bacteria in less than an hour of exposure. The hotter and wetter the environment, the more effective silver-coated fibres become. Apparel featuring these fibres also regulates temperature and minimises radiative heat loss by actively reflecting bodily energy back to the skin. In warm weather, the fibres cool the body by conducting heat from skin to ambient air.
Because silver is the most effective electromagnetic-interference (EMI) shielding element, silver-coated fibres are outstanding conductors of electricity. A few silver fibres are all that's needed to make a static-free product.

06

FLEXIBLE ELECTRONIC FABRIC

Composition
Conductive fibres woven into nylon

Properties
Soft surface, conductive, thin profile (1 mm), durable, shockproof, lightweight, flexible, cost competitive, versatile, conforms to irregular curved surfaces, washable, ranges in size from 2 cm to 2 metres

Applications
Mobile phones, computers, game consoles, automotive interiors, healthcare products

Contact
ElekSen
Pinewood Studios, Pinewood Road
Iver Heath
Buckinghamshire SL0 0NH
UK
T +44 (0)8700 727 272
incoming@eleksen.com
www.eleksen.com

Ideo
White Bear Yard
144a Clerkenwell Road
London EC1R 5DF
UK
T +44 (0)20 7713 2600
www.ideo.com

Logitech
6505 Kaiser Drive
Fremont CA 94555
USA
T +1 510 795 8500
www.logitech.com

Photo
The Soft Wrist Phone, designed by Ideo, does not force the user to talk into their wrist; the design allows the phone to be used as a familiar handset. The product creates a new technology; it is a watch when worn on the wrist, and a phone when held to the ear.

Although it looks and feels like an ordinary fabric, the flexible electronic fabric marketed as ElekTex incorporates a technology capable of electronic sensing, which makes it a so-called 'smart fabric'. The material combines conductive fabric structures with microchip technology. The electronics and software that are part of its soft surface create durable, lightweight interfaces. It can be folded, scrunched or wrapped as desired. This soft sensing technology is flexible, resilient, cost competitive, durable, versatile and lightweight, enabling previously hard consumer products to be made soft and user friendly. The first ElekTex-enabled commercial product is the Logitech KeyCase, an all-in-one keyboard and case that wraps around the hand-held unit when not in use to protect it from life on the road. A strong case of water-resistant fabric protects the PDA when travelling. The fabric structure can accurately sense location on three axes: X, Y and Z (Z being the amount of pressure applied to the 1-mm-thick material). ElekTex senses where the fabric is being pressed (X and Y axes) and how hard (via the Z axis). The precise electrical measurements are then translated into digital signals, which control the electronic device.

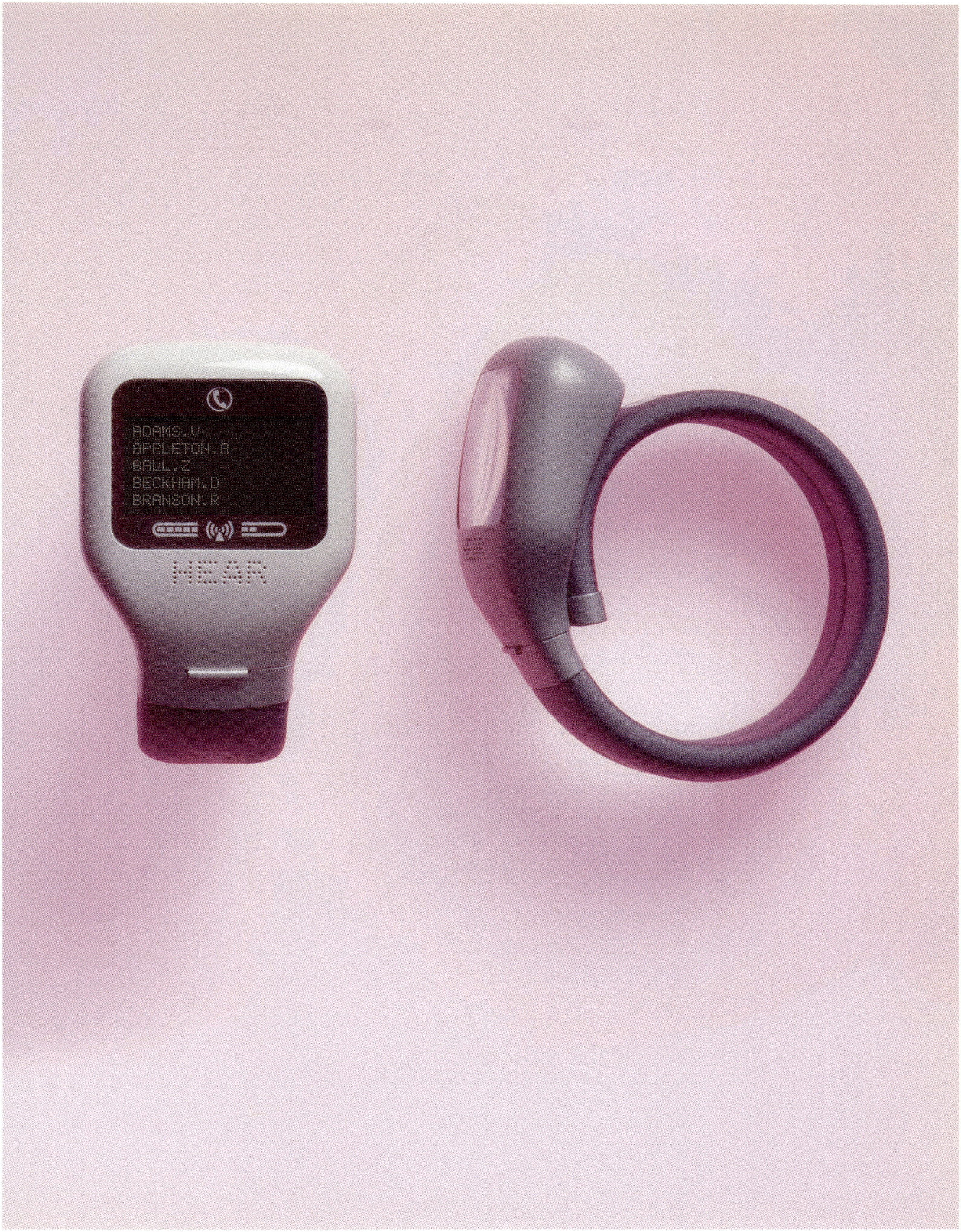
ADAMS.V
APPLETON.A
BALL.Z
BECKHAM.D
BRANSON.R
HEAR

07

SOLAR MODULES

Composition
Photovoltaic cells, polycarbonate sheets

Properties
Environmentally friendly, flexible, lightweight, durable, shapable both hot and cold, fire-resistance rating 1, (salt)waterproof, weatherproof, output up to 300Wp, heat insulation up to 1.2W/m2·K, sizes up to 100 x 300cm (special sizes available upon request)

Applications
Automotive and watercraft industries, lighting displays, architecture

Contact
Sunovation
Vital-Daelen-Strasse
D-63911 Klingenberg-Trennfurt
Germany
T +49 (0)9372 949 109
F +49 (0)9372 949 110
info@sunovation.de
www.sunovation.de

Photo
Solar modules consist of photo-voltaic cells elastically encapsulated between two sheets of polycarbonate.

One of tomorrow's main sources of solar energy is the photovoltaic cell, which converts sunlight directly into electricity. Sunovation's Solar Module features photovoltaic cells elastically encapsulated between two sheets of polycarbonate. A standard module consists of one or more cell clusters (36 multi-crystalline silicon cells make up one 10 x 10 cm cluster) and is only 8 to 10 mm thick. Interaction between sunlight and semiconductor (solar cell) produces a photovoltaic effect. In this process, electrical energy is released and conducted via metal contacts. The result is direct current.
Thanks to its extraordinary properties, the modular system is lightweight, strong, weatherproof and durable. The synthetic material is highly impact-resistant but significantly lighter than glass.
Standard modules are available in sizes up to 3 square metres. With the use of thermoforming, they can be shaped to achieve creative effects. During this process, the special 'floating' encapsulation system is moulded into any shape desired.
All necessary peripheral devices and power sources, such as lamps and light displays, can be integrated inconspicuously into the overall construction. This flexible material is being used to create various architecturally attractive features. Incorporated in a roof, for example, modules supply electricity for the illumination of doors and signs. Entrances, canopies, barrel vaults and multi-pitch roofs can all be simply equipped with solar modules, without changing the geometry of the structure in question. Solar modules can be integrated into illuminated strips and used to generate power for variable-speed motors (mechanical systems on islands). The modules can create a backup power supply and even produce solar current for the public mains.

08

ELECTRO-LUMINES-CENT FILM

Composition
Polyester film, phosphor ink, dielectric ink layers

Properties
Ultra-flat, flexible, unbreakable, uniform illumination of shaped and uneven surfaces, far-reaching light, clear graphics, diverse colours, shock- and vibration-resistant, anti-glare, free of UV and IR radiation, suitable for large surfaces, lightweight, extremely high luminous intensity possible, energy-saving, dimmable, flashing or continuous light, printable, expensive

Applications
Advertising, cinemas (stairs with integrated lighting stripes), theatre and opera, keyboards and instruments (aircraft, automotive), LCDs, indicators and emergency lighting (public areas), safety clothing (vests, belts), architecture and building, exhibitions, fairs, displays, promotion (stickers, frontlets, belts)

Contact
Light & Motion Lichttechnik
Paulusgasse 13
A-1030 Vienna
Austria
T +43 (0)171 423 26
F +43 (0)171 306 76
info@lightandmotion.at
www.lightandmotion.at

Photo
Electro-luminescent film is flexible and radiates light when connected to a power sorce.

Electro-luminescent film (EL film) is an active, luminous material. Electric voltage is all it needs to emit light. The film is ultra-thin, lightweight and extremely flexible. It can even be cut into the desired shape with a pair of scissors.
The product is made by screen-printing EL pastes onto a special grade of polyester film coated with indium tin oxide (ITO). Micro-encapsulated phosphors render the pastes damp-proof and extend their operating life. The phosphor ink is printed on polyester by means of a relatively simple silk-screen process, followed by the printing of two to three dielectric ink layers, a rear silver electrode ink and an encapsulation ink. This forms a capacitor structure that emits light when AC (±115 V) is applied. Thanks to light reflected in all directions, the use of EL film on clothing worn by cyclists, for example, is an excellent safety measure. The film radiates enough light to make the cyclist visible from a considerable distance. It can also be used as signage in places such as buildings and aeroplanes, and as lighting strips on stairways. Other applications are stage design or backlighting for automotive display and LCD panels. The unique features and good performance of electroluminescent lighting provide an alternative to the LEDs and incandescent and neon lamps used in industry. It can save space, reduce assembly of components and simplify design. The disadvantages of this material are the high price and the need for an inverter to operate the lamp; EL film works only on AC.

09

LIQUID-CRYSTAL WINDOWS

Composition
Laminated glass layered with oxide and liquid-crystal films

Properties
Turns milky white in response to an electrical charge (requires 10W/m2), transmits the same amount of light whether on or off, UV-proof, durable, easily maintained, eliminates need for curtains and blinds, hygienic, provides acoustic insulation. The product can be curved, silk-screen printed or sandblasted; is available in standard thicknesses of 11, 12 and 14 mm; comes in neutral, bronze, grey and green

Applications
Window or door panels, projection surfaces, automotive and transport sector (cars, buses, trains, planes)

Contact
Saint-Gobain Glass
Les Miroirs, 18, avenue d'Alsace
F-92096 La Défense 3 Cedex
France
T +33 (0)1 4762 3000
R.D@saint-gobain.com
www.saint-gobain.com

Photo
Indigo installation for Levi's Red Line, designed by Jurgen Bey for Droog Design. This installation – intended as a travelling display window – is composed of three display cases with liquid-crystal front panels that continuously switch from a translucent to a transparent state. Behind the glass, blue and white T bulbs change in intensity to the rhythm of the glass panels. Consequently, the clothing on display emerges from the coloured haze and sinks back into it, again to the beat of the liquid-crystal light show.

The polymer-dispersed liquid crystals (PDLCs) in switchable windows are based on a technology similar to that of LCDs. The liquid crystals used for windows respond to an electrical change with a parallel alignment that permits light to pass through. In the absence of an electrical charge, the liquid crystals are randomly oriented. Light entering the window has no clear path out, and the result is a translucent, milky white, glass surface. The technology works like this: two layers of film enclose a layer of tiny liquid crystals. This assembly is laminated between two pieces of heat-treated glass. Both faces of the film are covered with a transparent, electrically conductive metal coating. The coatings are wired to a power supply.
Liquid crystals either let all the light in or block all the light out. There are no intermediate settings, and the switch from one state to another is virtually instantaneous. Other than the diffusion of light, the optical properties of the two states are nearly identical; the window lets in approximately the same amount of light and solar energy whether on or off. Because there is little change in performance and because the windows require power to be transparent, this is not an energy-saving product.
As the basis of the first commercially available smart windows, PDLCs do not represent a developing technology. Used for privacy control, these windows are currently found in offices, public buildings, homes, buses, trains and planes. Saint-Roch markets the panels under the name Priva-Lite. PDLCs can be incorporated into multifunctional configurations, single or double glazing, safety glazing, thermal-insulation glazing, soundproof glazing and curved glass. PDLCs, which eliminate the need for curtains and blinds, are a functional and surprising alternative to, among other things, fitting-room and toilet doors (as seen at the Prada store in New York City). A translucent panel means the cubicle is occupied.

10

SELF-HEALING POLYMER

Composition
Modified epoxy resin, healing agent (dicyclopentadiene) and catalyst (Grubbs' catalyst)

Properties
Restores up to 75 per cent of initial strength

Applications
Deep-space vehicles, satellites, space stations, rocket motors, prosthetic organs, bridges

Contact
University of Illinois at Urbana-Champaign
Autonomic Healing Research Group
216 Talbot Lab, 104 S. Wright Street
Urbana IL 61801
USA
T +1 217 333 2322
F +1 217 244 5707
www.autonomic.uiuc.edu

Photo
Autonomic healing in action. Shown is a crack in an epoxy-polymer material. The crack plane runs along the bottom of the illustration. Red spheres are microcapsules containing a repair fluid dyed red. Following polymerisation, the fluid now fills part of the crack. Photo: Scott White et al.

Materials that mend themselves? Sounds pretty far-fetched. But a team at the University of Illinois has devised a biology-mimicking system that allows polymer composites to 'self-heal'. Early tests of their work show good results. Polymer composites are advanced materials consisting of two components: a reinforcing fibre and a liquid moulding resins. These materials may suffer damage caused by conditions like bond rupture, the formation of microvoids and fibres debonding from the resin through repeated usage.
The autonomic healing system is based on microcapsules 100 microns in diameter that are embedded in the epoxy polymer along with a special catalyst. When the polymer composite is damaged, the capsules pop open and release a healing agent (dicyclopentadiene or DCPD). At this point, contact between healing agent and catalyst produces polymerisation, which repairs the damage. The special microcapsule membrane ensures that catalyst and fluid meet only in the damaged zone. The healing agent restores up to 75 per cent of the initial strength of the composite material, thus giving it a life span two to three times longer than it would have had without the self-healing system. Minute cracks are mended before nature accelerates the process of deterioration provoked by moisture (swelling) and corrosion (cracking). Researchers foresee the application of this technology to other brittle materials, including various types of ceramics and glass.
The concept of self-healing composites has far-reaching consequences for product safety and reliability. The technology should prove especially useful in situations that preclude the reparation of a material after it has been put into use. Components of vehicles used in deep-space exploration, satellites, space stations, rocket motors and prosthetic organs are prime candidates for such treatment, as are innovative engineering projects like bridges constructed from composite materials.

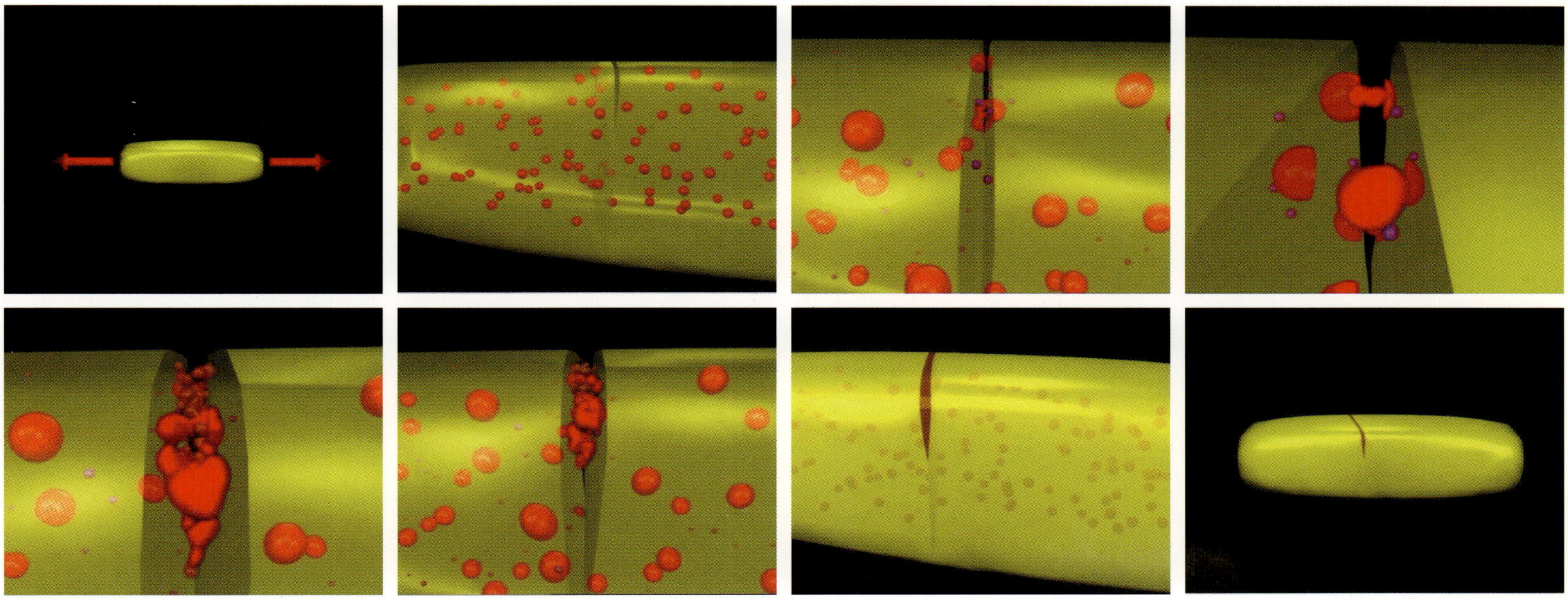

11

SELF-CLEANING GLASS

Composition
Glass coated with titanium oxide

Properties
Self-cleaning (24 hours a day, regardless of weather conditions), no polishing required, saves on window-cleaning products/services, environmentally friendly, durable, colourfast

Applications
Windows, façades and roofs, both residential and commercial; suitable for both vertical and angled glazing applications

Technical information
A video demonstration of the product can be seen at: www.pilkington.com/building/world/bpna/newsroom.html

Contact
Pilkington
Prescot Road
St. Helens WA10 3TT
UK
T +44 (0)1744 28 882
F +44 (0)1744 692 660
www.pilkington.com
www.activglass.com

Photo
Activ is a self-cleaning glass which relies on a hydophilic coating that absorbs UV rays to maintain its dirt-free surface.

Manufactured under the name Activ, this self-cleaning glass features a permanent coating of titanium oxide that repels dirt and grime. The microscopically thin coating is applied to the surface of the glass in its molten state. This technique makes the coating an integral part of the surface. The pyrolytic coating process increases product durability and prevents discolouration.
Activ works in two ways. It absorbs ultraviolet (UV) rays from the sun and, through a chemical reaction called catalysis, gradually but continuously loosens, breaks down and dissolves organic dirt. The coating is also hydrophilic, a quality that reduces the surface tension of water, causing it to run off the glass in sheets, washing away any dirt in its path, rather than to form droplets. A self-cleaning window, though nearly spotless, is constantly in the process of eliminating dirt from its surface.
It takes several days of exposure to UV light before the glass is activated. To achieve the full self-cleaning function, the glass should be left alone during this period. In regions with little rain, spraying the glass with water can activate the process. Even without water, however, the glass remains clean. After absorbing UV light for several days, the coated glass breaks down organic matter into carbon dioxide and water vapour.
Though Activ costs about 20 per cent more than traditional glazing, the advantages are numerous: it eliminates cleaning time, saves on window-cleaning products/services, protects the environment by reducing run-off of potentially harmful detergents, eliminates the need for ladders and industrial cleaning equipment operated at extreme heights, and stands up to the elements for over 20 years.

12

CLIMATE-CONTROL FABRIC

Composition
Fabric, foam featuring PCM-filled microcapsules

Properties
Climate control (prevents overheating and excessive cooling of the body), active breathing, moisture regulation, odourless, offers UV protection, weather resistant, crease resistant, can be washed, dry-cleaned and ironed

Applications
Clothing, shoes, gloves, upholstery and other textiles, medical products

Contact
Schoeller Textil
Bahnhofstrasse 17
CH-9475 Sevelen
Switzerland
T +41 (0)81 786 0800
F +41 (0)81 786 0810
info@schoeller-textiles.com
www.schoeller-textiles.com

Photo
Fabrics featuring phase change materials (PCMs) can store heat and emit it later, to protect the body from excessive cooling. The difference between heat storage in a jacket with and without climate-control fabric is clearly visible after a period of 45 minutes. The illustrations are the result of thermal photography.

The idea of a fabric that monitors body temperature is not new. To date, fabrics have regulated the fluid balance in the body, protected the body from wind and rain, and functioned in other passive ways. Schoeller Textil has developed a group of smart textiles – marketed as Schoeller-Comfor Temp – that feature active thermal regulation.
The product is based on phase change technology, which emerged from a 1980s NASA research programme. Its aim was to better protect instruments and astronauts against extreme fluctuations in temperature in outer space.
PCM is a collective term for materials capable of changing their physical state within a given range of temperature: from solid to liquid and vice versa. More than 500 natural and synthetic PCMs are known today. They differ from one another in terms of phase-change temperatures and heat-storage capacities.
Incorporating PCMs into textiles requires a process that captures the material within a protective wrapping, thus creating a microcapsule only several microns in diameter. The result is a fabric that does not leak during the liquid phase and that can withstand the effects of washing, dry-cleaning and weather-related stress.
When physical activity or a high ambient temperature causes body temperature to rise, the microcapsules react by absorbing heat.
The PCMs in the microcapsules melt. They draw in surrounding heat and store the surplus energy. When physical activity ceases or the ambient temperature falls, the PCMs solidify and the microcapsules emit the previously stored heat.
Temperature equalisation is maintained until all microcapsules have completed the phase change.
For textile applications, ideal carrier materials for PCM-filled microcapsules are fibres, coatings and foam. The thermal regulation of Schoeller-ComforTemp is provided by foam, which contains millions of these microcapsules: the more capsules carried by the foam, the more climate control provided by the fabric.

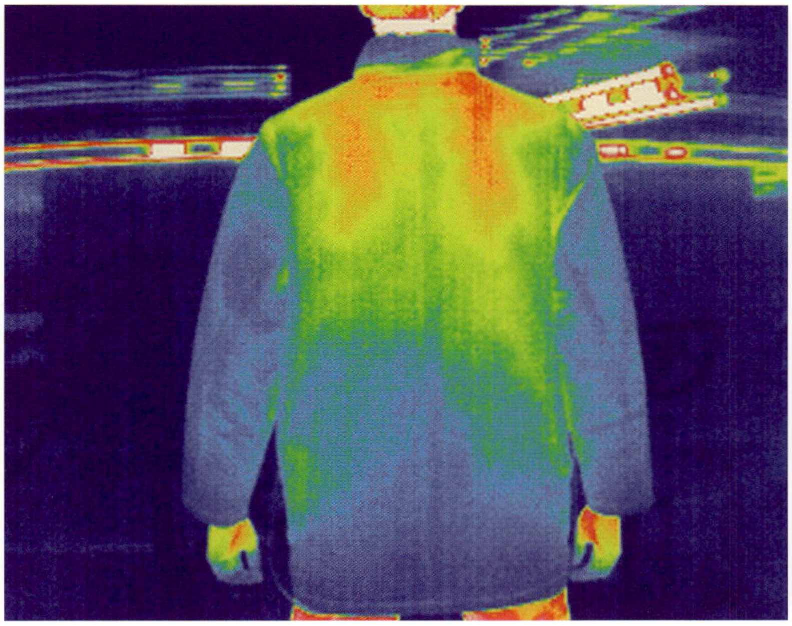

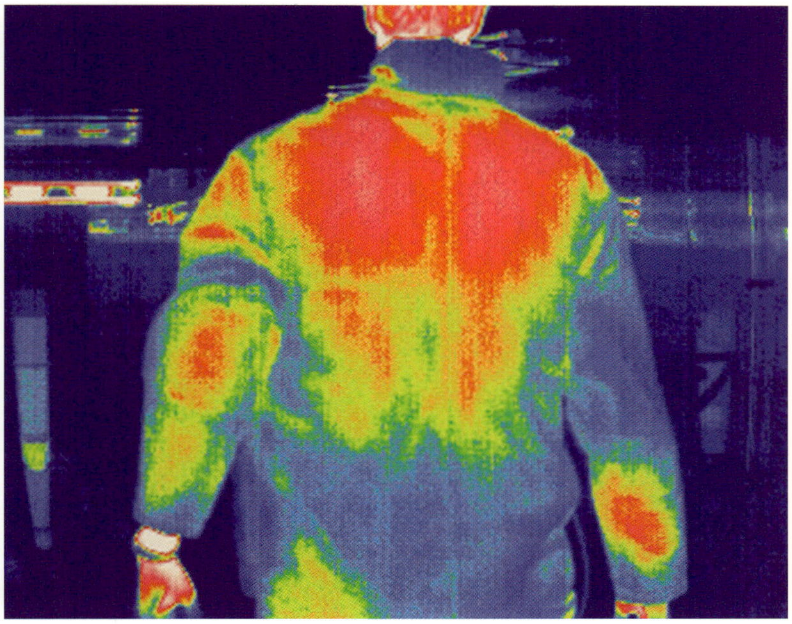

13

PIEZO-ELECTRIC CERAMICS

Composition
Lead zirconate titanate

Properties
Converts electrical energy to sound, motion, force or vibration – and vice versa

Applications
Ultrasonic air transducers, buzzers, speakers, alarms, disk and plate benders, igniters, actuators, nebuliser boards

Contact
American Piezo Ceramics
PO Box 180
Mackeyville PA 17750-0180
USA
T +1 570 726 6961
F +1 570 726 7466
apcsales@aol.com
www.americanpiezo.com

Photo
Piezoelectric ceramics can convert electrical energy into sound, motion, force or vibration – and vice versa.

Piezoelectric ceramics are made with crystalline materials (lead zirconate titanate, for example) that, when subjected to a light mechanica stress, can convert electrical energy into sound, motion, force or vibration and, conversely, can convert sound, motion, force or vibration into electrical energy. This makes them both sensors and reactors. Ceramics with piezoelectric properties are used in the electronics industry to make products like ultrasonic air transducers for proximity sensors, motion detectors, intruder alarms, and remote controls for buzzers and speakers. American Piezo Ceramics (APC) is involved in the development of Alumina/Zirconia ceramics, a long-life product highly resistant to thermal shock.
Other ongoing developments include the integration of piezoelectric ceramics into an intelligent system that adapts itself to changing environmental factors. The aerodynamic design of aircraft, for example, would benefit from a material for aeroplane wings that reacts to velocity by changing in volume or by altering the angle of the wings with respect to the fuselage. Piezoelectric materials have the potential to measure air currents and, using the resulting data, to adjust the rigidity and position of the wings. The development of such materials includes an earlier application, in which piezoelectric fibres were incorporated into a polymer film that can be laminated onto large building volumes. In the future, structures like bridges will be capable of recognising and repairing material defects without human intervention.

14

COLOUR-CHANGING PLASTIC

Composition
Plastic with micro-encapsulated thermochromatic substances

Properties
Temperature-based reversible colour change, compatible with nearly all thermoplastic materials, can be embossed

Disadvantage
Limited colour range

Applications
Plastic-moulded objects (spoons, stirrers, straws)

Contact
International Products & Services
Via Civesio 6
I-20097 San Donato Milanese (MI)
Italy
T +39 02 527 9641
F +39 02 523 0773
info@ips-srl.it
www.ips-srl.it

Photo
Objects made of colour-changing plastic react to variations in temperature.

Plastic-moulded objects change colour in response to temperature variations and sunlight. The technology is based on the encapsulation of tiny particles (in either a liquid or a solid state) within a thin membrane. The result is an aqueous microcapsule that preserves the physico-chemical properties of the encapsulated substance, allowing them to remain intact. The membrane can be provided with various properties. Microcapsules can be made resistant to external agents or sensitive to pressure, friction,humidity or heat. Variations in colour require predetermined temperatures between -25° and +58°C. Standard temperatures that cause changes in colour are: from 8° to 16°C (cold drinks and foodstuffs), from 24° to 33°C (body temperature) and from 40° to 50°C (warm drinks and foodstuffs). A limited scale of (reversible) colour changes is available. Applications include feeding spoons for infants, which change colour to show when food is too hot for the baby. Others are spoons or straws that change colour when they come into contact with ice cream.

NOW
AST
E

INTRO

It's been quite a while since the term 'innovative material' automatically pointed to the world of plastics. An increasing number of 'green' materials are entering the marketplace – products with properties once associated strictly with synthetics. Green materials combined with innovative manufacturing methods and attractive designs can lead to strong, durable products that do not reveal their alternative origins.
The next step involves injection-moulded biopolymers made of renewable resources. Biopolymers – even those that are completely biodegradable – have properties comparable to those of common plastics derived from oil. Scientists currently experimenting with a wide variety of biopolymers (based on products like potatoes, corn and lactic acid) are coming up with water- soluble products that include biode-gradable packaging for seeds and plants. Applications for these materials are endless. One intriguing idea is inexpensive garden furniture designed to last for one season, after which the environmentally conscious user can toss it on the compost pile.

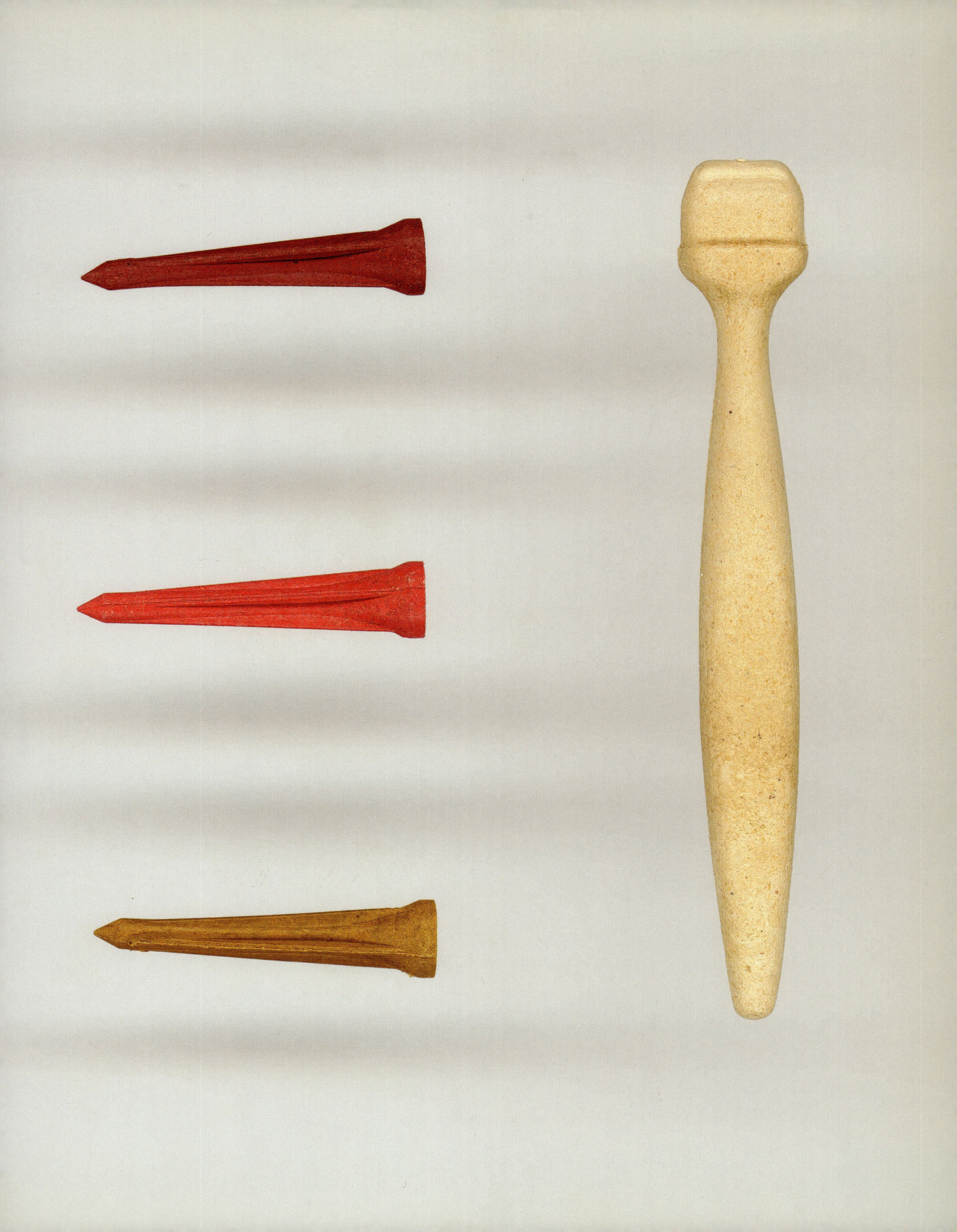

WWW.TREEPLAST.COM
SKIPSTONE
ORIGINAL

15

THERMO-PLASTIC WOOD

Composition
Organic materials such as wood chips, corn flour and plant resins

Properties
Fully biodegradable, wood-like appearance, suitable for injection moulding, serves as an alternative for plastic, available in a water-resistant version, non-electrostatic, shrink-free

Applications
Toys, gifts, ballistic projectiles, packaging, skirting boards, indoor furniture, agricultural uses

Technical specifications
www.treeplast.com/technical_specifications.htm

Contact
Treeplast
PE Design and Engineering
PO Box 3051
NL-2601 DB Delft
The Netherlands
T +31 (0)15 214 3420
F +31 (0)15 214 3323
info@treeplast.com
www.treeplast.com

Photo
Treeplast is a biopolymer composed of wood, corn and plant resins. It has been used to make a handy, biodegradable golf tee.

Thermoplastic wood, marketed as Treeplast, is a biopolymer made of wood chips (50 per cent), crushed corn and plant resins. The raw materials are extruded to make Treeplast granules, which can be processed in conventional plastic-processing machines. Treeplast is a good alternative for plastics manufacturers that want to carry a line of natural, biodegradable products without investing in new machinery. It is available in several versions, including a fully biodegradable version (several hours in water, four to six weeks outdoors) and a water-resistant version (several months). The advantage of Treeplast over other biopolymers is its wood-like appearance and texture, qualities that visually convey the organic nature of the material. It looks and feels like wood, but it can be shaped and moulded with far greater freedom than one has when working with wood. The final product can be finished like wood and is comparable, in terms of application, to MDF. Because it is biodegradable, Treeplast is suitable for a wide range of applications. One example is the golf tee. After teeing off, the golfer doesn't have to spend precious time looking for the tee. Thanks to precipitation in all its guises, the biodegradable tee eventually dissolves, leaving only a few particles of wood fibre in the grass.

16

PALM FLOORING

Composition
Coconut-palm wood, ceramic finish

Properties
Organic, helps reduce depletion of rainforests, uses an eco-friendly manufacturing process, is dark- to medium-mahogany in colour

Application
Flooring

Contact
Smith & Fong Company
375 Oyster Point Blvd. #3
San Francisco CA 94080
USA
T +1 650 872 1184
F +1 650 872 1185
webmaster@durapalm.com
www.durapalm.com

Photo
A highly durable material, palm-wood flooring is made of a by-product formerly discarded after coconuts were harvested.

As the rainforest continues to be tapped for much of the timber used in Asia, coconut palms have been an overlooked and under-utilised resource, as were rubber trees in the past. Coconut plantations have long been valued for the production of coconuts and their by-products: husks and shells. Not for wood. Palms produce for 60 to 80 years before becoming sterile. Unproductive trees are removed and replaced with saplings. Palm wood used for products made by DuraPalm comes from coconut plantations in Southeast Asia. Zero-VOC (volatile organic compounds) adhesives are used to produce this durable, quality floor covering. Approximately 2 cm thick, engineered palm flooring is harder than rock maple and exceptionally stable. Various trim mouldings are available.

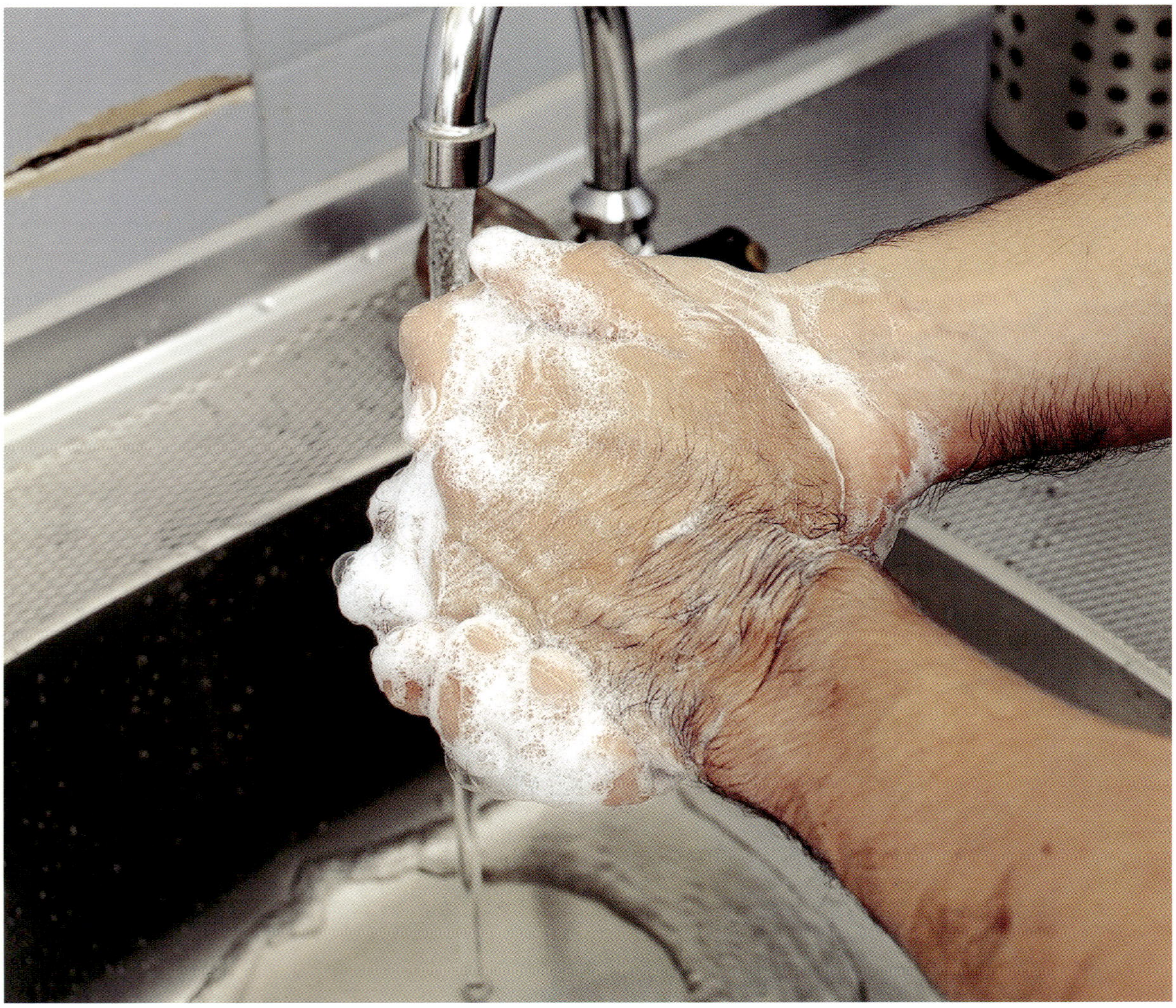

17

BIO-DEGRADABLE PLASTICS

Composition
Organic products such as whey, lactic acid, potatoes and wood

Properties
Dissolves or otherwise biodegrades within a certain period of time, can be programmed to release nutriments or odours, can be used as an alternative for conventional plastics

Applications
A wide variety, from bones for dogs to blister packs

Contact
B!PP Creative Facility
PO Box 6241
NL-5600 HE Eindhoven
The Netherlands
T +31 (0)40 296 2415
F +31 (0)40 296 2416
wsww.bipp.nl
www.biopolymer.net

Photo
Leafz is the brand name of small boxes containing wafer-thin leaves of soap. Made of polylactic acid, the translucent, boxes are biodegradable.

The term biopolymer refers to any polymer made of fully biodegradable and/or reusable organic substances. Certain biopolymers are produced by the biological systems of micro-organisms, plants and animals; others are chemically synthesised from organic materials like sugars, starches, natural fats and oils. Most biopolymers are biodegradable. Some are water-soluble. Most can be composted and/or addec to landfill sites. Biodegradation times vary from a couple of days to years. Biopolymers are the alternative to petroleum-based polymers or traditional plastics. They are suitable for many applications, from packaging and bottles to car parts and nappies. Dutch firm B!pp, for example, used the material to develop Leafz: small boxes containing wafer-thin leaves of soap. Made of polylactic acid, the translucent, biodegradable boxes can be composted when empty. The firm is currently working on BulbScrew, a tulip-bulb planter made of potato starch. The product has a futuristic, screw-shaped body that facilitates planting, even determining the exact underground depth required to produce healthy tulips. B!pp is also researching potential additions to the planter, options that would become effective as or after precipitation dissolves the starch. Options include nutriments to aid plant growth and odorous substances designed to repel rodents and other pests.

18

RECYCLED POLYETHYL-ENE

Composition
Polyethylene

Properties
Nontoxic, eco-friendly, aesthetic, available in various colours or combinations of colours, boasts unique patterns, can be formed into curved objects

Applications
Laminates or solid-surfacing materials (indoors and out), furniture, retail and exhibition design, restroom and shower partitions, screens, walls, translucent light diffusion, various art- and design-related uses

Technical specifications
www.yemmhart.com/materials/origins/specifications.htm

Contact
Yemm & Hart
1417 Madison 308
Marquand MO 63655-9153
USA
T +1 573 783 5434
F +1 573 783 7544
info@yemmhart.com
www.yemmhart.com

Deutsche Gesellschaft für Kunststoff-Recycling
Frankfurterstrasse 720-726
D-51145 Cologne
Germany
T +49 (0)2203 931 7743
F +49 (0)2203 931 7828
www.dkr.de

Photo
Recycled polyethylene is made of post-consumer polyethylene packaging; patterns and motifs completely penetrate the plastic.

Made wholly of post-consumer polyethylene packaging, this multi-coloured plastic offers an aesthetic response to recycling that is not dull and dutiful but enthusiastic. It can be used as a laminate or a solid-surfacing material, which makes it a good alternative to traditional plastics and wood. Because each product is made of a different blend of components, no two products are alike. Unlike plastic laminates with repetitive patterns, recycled-polyethylene products are based on a random quality that makes each result unique. Colours completely penetrate the material, an obvious benefit to both designer and manufacturer. Safe and nontoxic, recycled polyethylene is an eco-friendly product that helps minimise waste. Plastic bottles are collected, sorted by colour and shredded into oatmeal-size flakes that are rinsed in hot water to remove contaminates and then dried thoroughly. Sorting bottles by colour during the preparation phase allows manufacturers to offer clients custom-coloured products.
American firm Yemm & Hart manufactures Origins, a line of products based on recycled polyethylene. Origins includes a series of decorative panels that can be used as laminates or as a solid-surfacing material. Colour-chart options speak for themselves: confetti, rainforest, carnival and cool splash are nice examples. The minimum flake size is 3.175 mm. Various sheet sizes and thicknesses are available (± 0.3 to 5 cm). The standard mat finish is scratch-resistant.
The German Society for Plastic Recycling (DKR) has developed a line of interior-design products that takes advantage of recycled polyethylene. The DKR is not a recycling agency; it receives 'Green Dot' packaging from Dual System sorting plants and passes it on to contract partners for further recycling. In collaboration with designers of furniture, light objects, screens and washbasins, DKR organises the development of a wide range of products. Though made in series production, each product is composed of a blend of different components and each is unique.

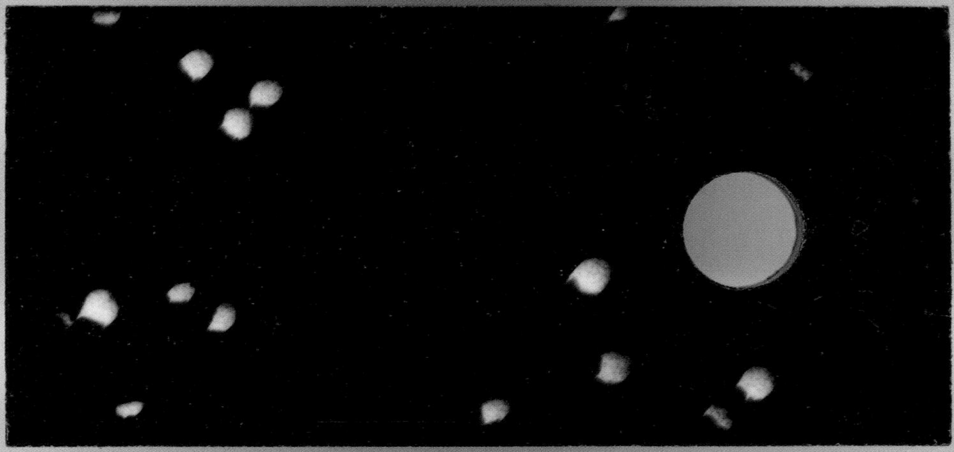

OPT
ICAL
EFF
ECT
S

INTRO

Glittering ceilings, fluorescent walls, an interactive light floor, furnishings with magical chromatic effects . . . Are we experiencing a revival of the disco glamour that marked the seventies and eighties? A flashback of the spectacle and grandeur of old casinos, clubs and theatres? Take one look at the impressive range of materials with special colour, light and see-through effects and it's obvious: optical surprises are hot. Sommers Plastic, 3M, BASF and others have come up with various films, pigments and fabrics that allow designers to play with optical effects like the iridescent look of a butterfly wing. HoloPro is another interesting material. When it is applied to glass, the surface can be used for holographic projections visible on one side only. Used on a display window, HoloPro invites passers-by to view films projected on the outer surface, while shoppers inside see nothing but a transparent window. Another illusory effect is produced by Lumisty film, which reflects light or lets it pass through, depending on the angle of incidence. A window-stopper for the window-shopper.

Designers are having a field day with these innovative materials. Matt Sindall uses light and lenticular surfaces to realise colour changes in his work. Equally innovative are Gruppe Re's fluorescent glass tiles, which rely on luminous pigment for their special look. The pigment collects UV rays from natural or artificial light and releases them after dark in the form of a bright greenish-yellow light. Sometimes designers come up with new applications for existing materials. Reflecting film and tape were initially reserved for emergency vehicles, street signs and road workers' clothing. Dutch project group STIP rewrites the story on retro-reflecting prismatic foil by applying it to the façades of new post offices in the Netherlands, which are now visible at night.

Optical effects sometimes go beyond cosmetic design to put the fun in functional.

19

COLOUR-SHIFTING THERMO-PLASTIC FILM

Composition
PVC, polyester, acrylic

Properties
Exhibits colour-shifting effects, suitable for lamination and embossing

Applications
Cosmetics packaging, footwear, sporting goods, handbags, wallpaper

Contact
Sommers Plastic Products
81 Kuller Road
Clifton NJ 07015
USA
T +1 973 777 7888
F +1 973 345 1586
sales@sommers.com
www.sommers.com

Photo
The layered construction of Mystery Mirror thermoplastic sheets causes colour-shifting effects.

Mystery Mirror is a thermoplastic sheet that exhibits colour-shifting effects. It is composed of two polyvinyl chloride (PVC) sheets laminated onto either side of a multi-layered film consisting of over 300 polyester/acrylic layers. The layered construction causes interference and absorption of light and both refracts and transmits different colours depending on the viewing angle and the light source. The sheet, which may be laminated or embossed, is available in two colourways (cyan/purple and gold/magenta), in a firm or soft hand, in various gauges and grains (foil, feather stretch, white patent) and in sheets of 60 x 136 cm or rolls 61cm wide.

20

DECORATIVE WIRE GLASS

Composition
Glass, stainless steel

Properties
Translucent, tactile, creates an optical effect, prevents shattering in the event of breakage

Applications
Partition walls, secondary glazing, shower cubicles, tabletops

Contact
Loods 5 Ontwerpers
Generaal Bothastraat 5k
NL-5642 NJ Eindhoven
The Netherlands
T +31 (0)40 281 2000
loods5@chello.nl

Photo
The reinforcement featured in decorative wire glass creates striking visual effects.

Decorative wire glass is founded glass to which a piece of stainless-steel webbing has been added. The 3-D effect is intensified by combining the stainless-steel reinforcement with figured glass featuring a low-relief surface pattern. The play of light and a barely perceptible background determine the appearance of this innovative product. Because the material does not shatter when broken, it also functions as safety glass.
The reinforcement in conventional wire glass is kept as inconspicuous as possible by polishing the stainless-steel wire to make it less visible. After designer Simone de Waart discovered the optical quality of the wire, however, she decided to highlight the reinforcement by using it in a visibly aesthetic manner. Standard wire glass with a ribbed structure, for example, has a fascinating spiral effect. Ridges refract the light, making the thick, flat standard wire visible in some places and invisible in others. This effect occurs only when the ridges are at a certain angle in relation to the wire.
The search for new types of reinforcement also led to the development of industrial finds (such as metal filters used in the food industry) into usable and playful structures.
Loods 5 Ontwerpers created its purpose-designed, plate-glass product for specific interior-design and architecture projects. In each case, dimensions (including thickness), patterns and structures were determined by the project in question.

21

LED LIGHT PANELS

Composition
Glass or acrylic, LEDs, imprinted dotted pattern

Properties
Provides evenly distributed light, available in all RGB colours, continuous adjustment, low-energy, produces almost no heat, durable, dimensions of up to w1500 x h3500 mm, various thicknesses (6 to 19 mm), available as insulated glass, single-sheet glass and curved glass

Applications
Architecture (including existing buildings), ceilings, walls, floors, safety and signage systems for public space, products, furniture

Contact
Emdelight
Otto-Strasse 7
D-50859 Köln
Germany
T +49 (0)2234 690 530
F +49 (0)2234 690 528
info@emdelight.com
www.emdelight.com

Photo
The Light & Easy table, designed and manufactured by Emdelight, features built-in LEDs capable of changing colour. Photography by Constantin Meyer.

Using LED technology, manufacturer Emdelight has developed light panels capable of producing all colours of the RGB spectrum. Made of either glass or acrylic, the panels are imprinted with a dotted pattern. Each dot acts as an 'intended diversion point', which allows light to exit the panel. The specially designed pattern provides a uniform distribution of light. LEDs are concealed within the angle sections of the framework. The concept makes lighting an integral part of architecture and interior design rather than a separate element. The colour and intensity of the light can be adapted to the mood of the user, as well as to the type of daylight entering the space. Not only can the panel change colour; a single panel can also include more than one colour. (A panel that is red on one side and yellow on the other, for example, also displays every shade of orange that appears between these two primary colours on the spectrum.)
LEDs are virtually unbreakable, individually adjustable and durable (with a life span of over 100,000 hours). They produce almost no heat and use very little energy. The ceramic colours imprinted on Emdelight panels are bonded to the surface through an enamelling process. These abrasion-proof, non-fade colours are highly resistant to acid, lye and temperature variations. The printed area covers about 10 to 15 per cent of the surface of the panel. Emdelight panels are available in dimensions of up to 1500 x 3500 mm and in thicknesses from 6 to 19 mm. Options include insulated, single- sheet and curved glass. Architectural applications for the versatile product range from façades, parapets and roofs to partition walls, ceilings, floors and stairs. The panels are also suitable for furniture and product design.

22

LENTICULAR FILM WITH CHROMATIC EFFECT

Composition
Polyester

Properties
Refractive, flexible, has a prismatic structure, creates a chromatic effect

Applications
Furniture, interior surface finishes

Contact
Matt Sindall
8 bis, rue de la Baume
F-75008 Paris
France
T +33 (0)1 4359 6413
M +33 (0)6 0790 9296
msindall@noos.fr

Photo
Designer Matt Sindall collaborated with Roger Tallet to create a chair clad in lenticular film (a refractive film mounted on a printed layer of coloured lines). Their chromatic chair appears to change colour as the viewing angle changes.

In looking for a surface treatment for a chair, designer Matt Sindall disregarded the inert and static in favour of something with multiple levels of perception. Direct inspiration came from the lenticular printing process used for the 'moving' pictures on Pokémon cards. The same process has also been used to animate billboard images. In collaboration with Parisian Roger Tallet, Sindall mounted a refractive film (type 3M) onto a printed layer of green, blue and red lines. The result was a chromatic effect; the lenticular film appeared to play with the colour spectrum.
Sindall and Tallet created the effect by juxtaposing several microprisms that are visible in gradation depending on the viewing angle. Position the refractive film a fraction of a millimetre to the right or left, and the chromatic effect disappears.
Having produced several of these panels, Sindall and Tallet cut them up to clad a chair made of 5-mm-thick plywood. Their 'chromatic chair' – a simply designed and universally recognisable archetype – reacts to the time of day and to the type of light that strikes it. Look at the chair from different angles and watch it alter in appearance. Three linear definitions are available: 144, 75 and 45 lines per inch. In this design, the optical effect takes precedence over ergonomics, comfort and shape.

23

3-D OBJECTS IN POLYMER

Composition
Polymer resin

Properties
Hand-cast, translucent, suitable for backlighting, requires standard woodworking tools, can be re-polished and/or cleaned with any non-abrasive household cleaner

Applications
Surfaces, feature walls, light fixtures, inset details in cabinetry and furniture

Contact
Skyline design
1240 North Homan Avenue
Chicago IL 60651
USA
T +1 773 278 4660
F +1 773 278 3548
sales@skydesign.com
www.skydesign.com

Photo
Lumicast decorative panels consist of three-dimensional objects (shown is Asian grass) captured in clear polymer.

A series of hand-cast decorative panels consisting of three-dimensional objects captured in clear polymer is marketed under the name Lumicast. Having clear or frosted finishes, these translucent panels are dramatic whether lit from back or front. Standard thickness is 1.91 cm, but the material can be custom fabricated for specific applications. Available in sizes up to 60.96 x 182.88 cm, Lumicast works best in a modular or grid format. The panels can be used in the same way and in the same locations as standard acrylic products. Normal woodworking tools may be used to make alterations to the material. Most three-dimensional objects not exceeding 1.59 cm in thickness will work successfully in a Lumicast panel.

24

BEADED SURFACE MATERIAL

Composition
Glass beads, aluminium composite material, fluorocarbon paint

Properties
Shimmering surface, scratch- and fire-resistant, durable

Applications
Public spaces (walls, ceilings, elevator panels, columns, signage, decorative trim)

Technical specifications
Downloads via www.forms-surfaces.com/products/silver_screen/index.html

Contact
Surfaces+ (Forms+Surfaces)
6395 Cindy Lane
Carpinteria CA 93013
USA
T +1 877 626 7788
F +1 805 684 8620
marketing@forms-surfaces.com
www.forms-surfaces.com

Photo
Silver Screen relies on an aluminium composite material clad in glass beads for its glistening, luminescent surface.

Silver Screen is a surface material with a shimmering, luminescent look. It features 2-mm, technical-grade glass beads on an aluminium composite backing clad in a durable coat of white fluorocarbon paint. Light splashes and ricochets off the spheres, creating a lively, shimmering surface. When underlaid with colour, graphics, murals or logos, the pearlescent spheres become a personalised and dramatic spatial expression.
The material is suitable for the enhancement of busy commercial spaces, such as casinos, clubs, hotels and bars. Dramatic lighting produces a glamorous, almost ethereal glow. Spotlights, coloured beams and projected still or moving images can be used with Silver Screen to create special effects, such as twinkling ceilings, curvaceous forms and glittering walls.
The material cannot be used as a structural building element, and it is not designed to reinforce or brace structural members. Silver Screen is 0.48 cm thick and comes in 152.4-x-274.32 cm sheets. A panelled version is also available.

25

INTERACTIVE LIGHT FLOOR

Composition
Sandwich construction of floorgrade glass, scratch-resistant plastic and an unguent, coloured fluid; light installation

Properties
Strong, scratch-resistant, interactive, all colours of light and fluid available, surface size unlimited

Applications
Flooring in interior and exterior public facilities, from bars, restaurants and waiting rooms to cinemas and entrances to office buildings; direction indicators in department stores and airports

Contact
Rogier Sterk
Apeldoornsestraat 14
NL-6828 AB Arnhem
The Netherlands
T +31 (0)26 445 1600
r.sterk@tiscali.nl

Photo
A pedestrian's footprints remain visible for about a minute after crossing the interactive light floor designed by Rogier Sterk.

The sandwich construction of this interactive light floor has a top layer of scratch-resistant plastic, a bottom layer (3-cm-thick) of floor-grade glass and, directly beneath the surface of the floor, a middle layer of coloured fluid in the form of a thin film. The sandwich construction rests on a supporting structure that accommodates a light installation. The weight of someone walking across the floor displaces some or most of the fluid, leaving 'light prints' wherever the foot touches the surface. Though these prints vanish as the pedestrian proceeds, it takes about a minute for them to disappear completely – turning around, he sees the trail of his own footsteps. The floor currently in use requires a supporting structure with a depth of about 30 cm. Future projects will rely on LED tiles only 3 cm thick and, consequently, on a supporting structure just 5 cm deep. The effect will be comparable to that of a light box. The tiles will have the same dimensions as the standard glass tiles now in use.
When supported by the transparent floor of an intermediate storey, the product can perform without built-in light. Here the pedestrian makes see-through footprints that reveal what is happening downstairs. And when the people below look up, they see a uniformly coloured ceiling interrupted by the same transparent footprints.

26

COLOUR-VARIABLE PIGMENT

Composition
Flat particles of aluminium or iron-oxide pigment, silicon oxide, iron oxide

Properties
Colour-variable, available as powder

Applications
Automotive finishes, industrial paints, powder coatings, coil coatings, plastics

Technical specifications
PDF-downloads via www.basf.de

Contact
BASF Aktiengesellschaft
Marketing World Pigments
Carl-Bosch-Strasse 38
D-67056 Ludwigshafen
Germany
T +49 (0)621 607 2361
F +49 (0)621 607 2869
info.service@basf-ag.de
www.basf.de

Photo
Articles coloured with Variocrom pigments vary in colour when viewed from different angles.

Variocrom is a colour-variable pigment; surfaces to which it is applied vary in colour when viewed from different angles. The phenomenon of a new colour at every turn is known as the 'flop effect'. Colour-variable pigments contain tiny flat particles of aluminium or iron oxide with diameters of 15 to 100 micro-metres and thicknesses of 300 to 500 nanometres. The particles receive a series of coatings, beginning with a thin film of silica with a low refractive index, which is followed by layers of reflective materials. Light absorption and reflection produce the desired effect. Three chromatic gradations are available: purple to gold, pink to yellow and greenish gold to reddish grey. Combining Variocrom with conventional pigments enhances the flop effect.
Nature provided the inspiration for this material; think of a shimmering butterfly wing or the shell of a beetle. Researchers captured the effect in a coating that both reflects and refracts light. Applications include industrial paints (an example is the automotive industry), powder coatings and coil coatings. Variocrom pigments can also be used to colour the plastics used in cosmetics packaging, decorative foil, synthetic leather, sports articles, trim in car interiors and so forth. Nail polish is another promising application.

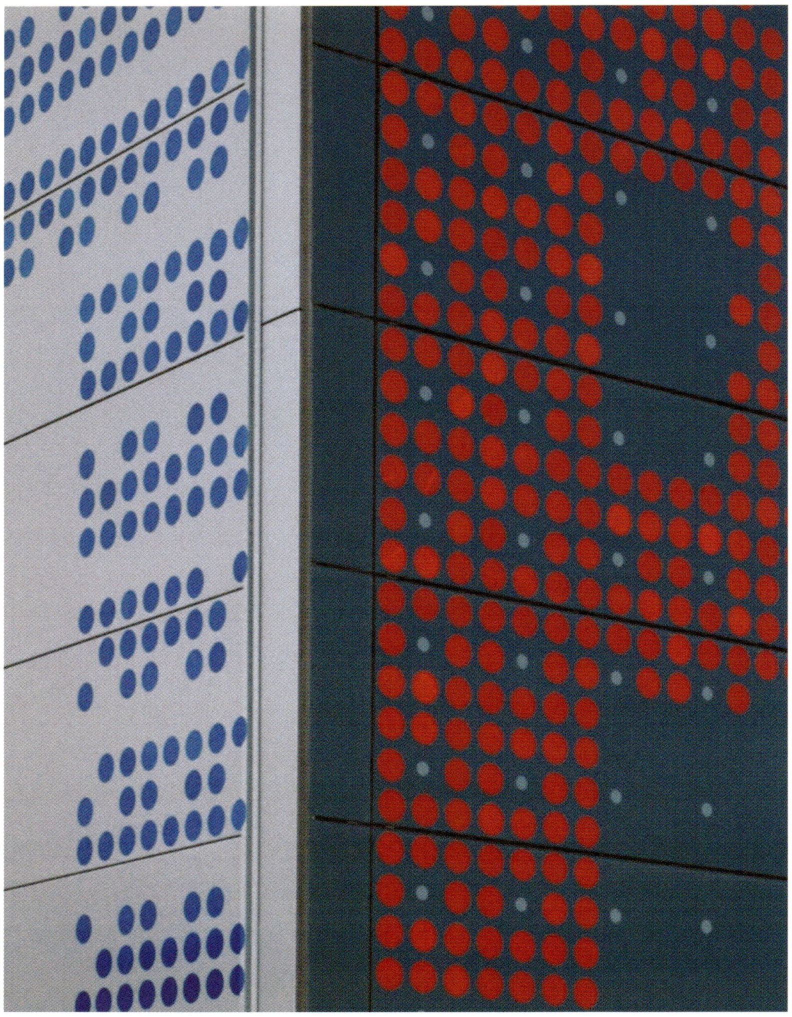

27

RETRO-REFLECTING PRISMATIC FILM

Composition
Polyester, PSA adhesive

Properties
Reflective, high degree of brightness, easily removable, no edge sealing required, wide colour range (including fluorescent yellow and orange)

Applications
Vehicles (police and emergency), architectural surfaces

Contact
Reflexite Europa
Lyngsoe Allé 3
DK-2970 Hoersholm
Denmark
T +45 (0)45 761 122
F +45 (0)45 761 102
europe@reflexite.com
www.reflexite-europe.com

Neon Weka
Molenkade 50-51
NL-1115 AC Duivendrecht
The Netherlands
T +31 (0)20 695 1151
F +31 (0)20 695 2241
rob.nolte@neonweka.nl

STIP – System Typography
Integrated Program
Buro Lange Haven (BLH)
Lange Haven 80
NL-3111 CH Schiedam
The Netherlands
T +31 (0)10 473 8089
F +31 (0)10 473 7408
info@blh.nl

Photo
The façade of a Dutch post office displays the dot matrix of Reflexite Daybright, a retro-reflecting prismatic film. Photography by STIP.

Reflexite Europa bases its line of reflecting film and tape on prismatic technology, which includes the dispersion, reflection and deviation of light. In the case of retro-reflecting prismatic film, light strikes each of the three surfaces of a microprism in turn before returning to its source. The precise arrangement of the microprisms enhances the efficiency of the product. A highly economical use of surface area delivers an optimum degree of reflection.
A case study done for the Dutch postal system demonstrated the success of this material as an architectural resource. PTT Post required a universal visibility system for its post offices. Buro Lange Haven teamed up with Neon Weka to establish a separate company devoted exclusively to this project: System Typography Integrated Programme (the abbreviation, STIP, is the Dutch word for 'dot'). The result was the '100 Dots Project', a matrix of red and white dots of retro- reflecting prismatic film with a standard diameter of 75 mm, which covers the entire façade. Different sizes and variations of the ball matrix were used to reproduce the colours of the PTT logo. The vocabulary thus created provides a database for the design of each building. The logo is applied to the galvanised-steel and glazed façade of each post office.
The retro-reflecting foil that composes the dots uses daylight to give each building and its logo an extra dimension. At night the foil does the same with artificial light, including light strips installed on the façade. The dipped headlights of oncoming cars are another source of reflection. This visibility system can be applied to any smooth surface; neon signs and illumination masts are unnecessary.
The dots that form the matrix of the design are manufactured in continuous rolls and cut out using lettering stencils. The dots are small enough to create a clearly perceptible image close up and large enough to produce a monumental image when viewed from a distance.
The polyester film used for this project is Reflexite Daybright.

28

SPECIAL-EFFECTS THERMO-PLASTICS

Composition
Polycarbonate (Lexan), ABS/PC (Cycolac and Cycoloy)

Properties
Easy to use (injection moulding), chromatic and optical effects present in the raw material (pellets), no extra coating required, cost-effective

Applications
Computers and other office equipment, flooring, mobile phones, automotive products, toys, appliances, cosmetics

Technical specifications
www.geplastics.com/resins/visualfx

Contact
GE Plastics
Pittsfield MA
USA
T +1 413 448 7569
www.geplastics.com

Photo
Visualfx plastics require no additional paints or coatings thanks to chromatic and optical effects in the raw material.

Visualfx is an extensive range of decorative resins created by fashion and aesthetics forecaster Bureau de Style Peclers of Paris. Resins with a mother-of-pearl, metal-flake or frosted look add a visual dimension to the design of consumer products like printers and mobile phones. Thanks to special chromatic and optical effects present in the raw material (pellets), injection moulding produces colourful, attractive components that require no additional paint or coating. The plastics used are based on polycarbonate (Lexan) and ABS/PC (Cycolac and Cycoloy) resins. Examples of the Visualfx collection are Light Diffusion, Make-Up, Intrigue Angular Metamerism, Enyo and Illuminate. Light Diffusion uses light to produce a sense of depth and mystery. Make-Up relies on rich colour and a touch of sparkle (created by a fine metallic flake) for its voluptuous opaque sheen. Intrigue Angular Metamerism features a two-tone colour-shifting effect that results in a three-dimensional look. Enyo moves dramatically through a spectrum of colour as the viewing angle changes, accompanied by an impression of tiny crystals. Illuminate is a translucent resin with a brilliant 'edge glow' effect. GE Plastics has provided the multifaceted Visualfx programme with its own design studio and three Special Effects service centres located in the Netherlands, the United States and China.

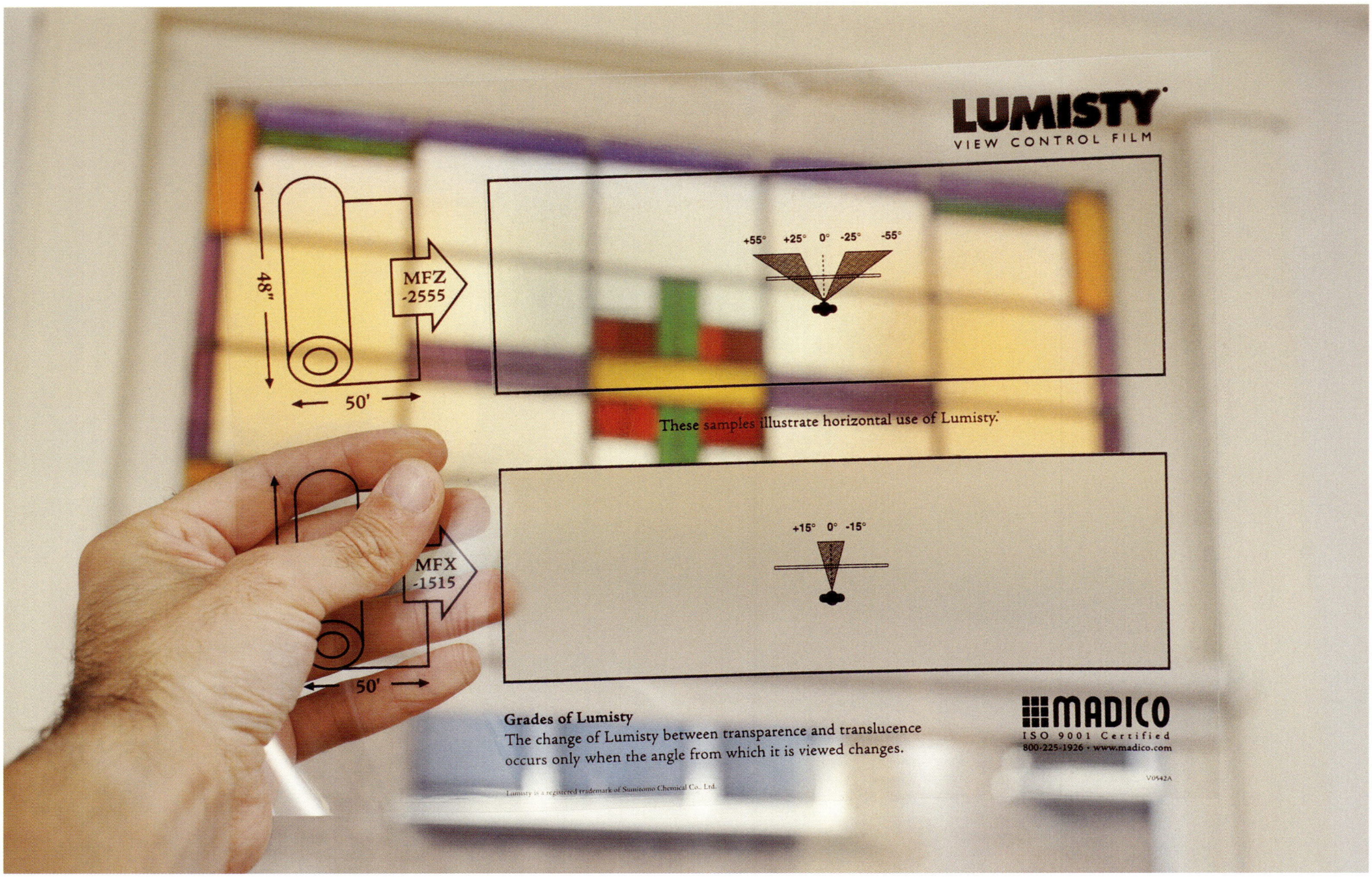
LUMISTY
VIEW CONTROL FILM
48"
MFZ
-2555
50'
+55° +25° 0° -25° -55°
These samples illustrate horizontal use of Lumisty.
+15° 0° -15°
MFX
-1515
50'
Grades of Lumisty
The change of Lumisty between transparence and translucence occurs only when the angle from which it is viewed changes.
Lumisty is a registered trademark of Sumitomo Chemical Co., Ltd.
MADICO
ISO 9001 Certified
800-225-1926 • www.madico.com

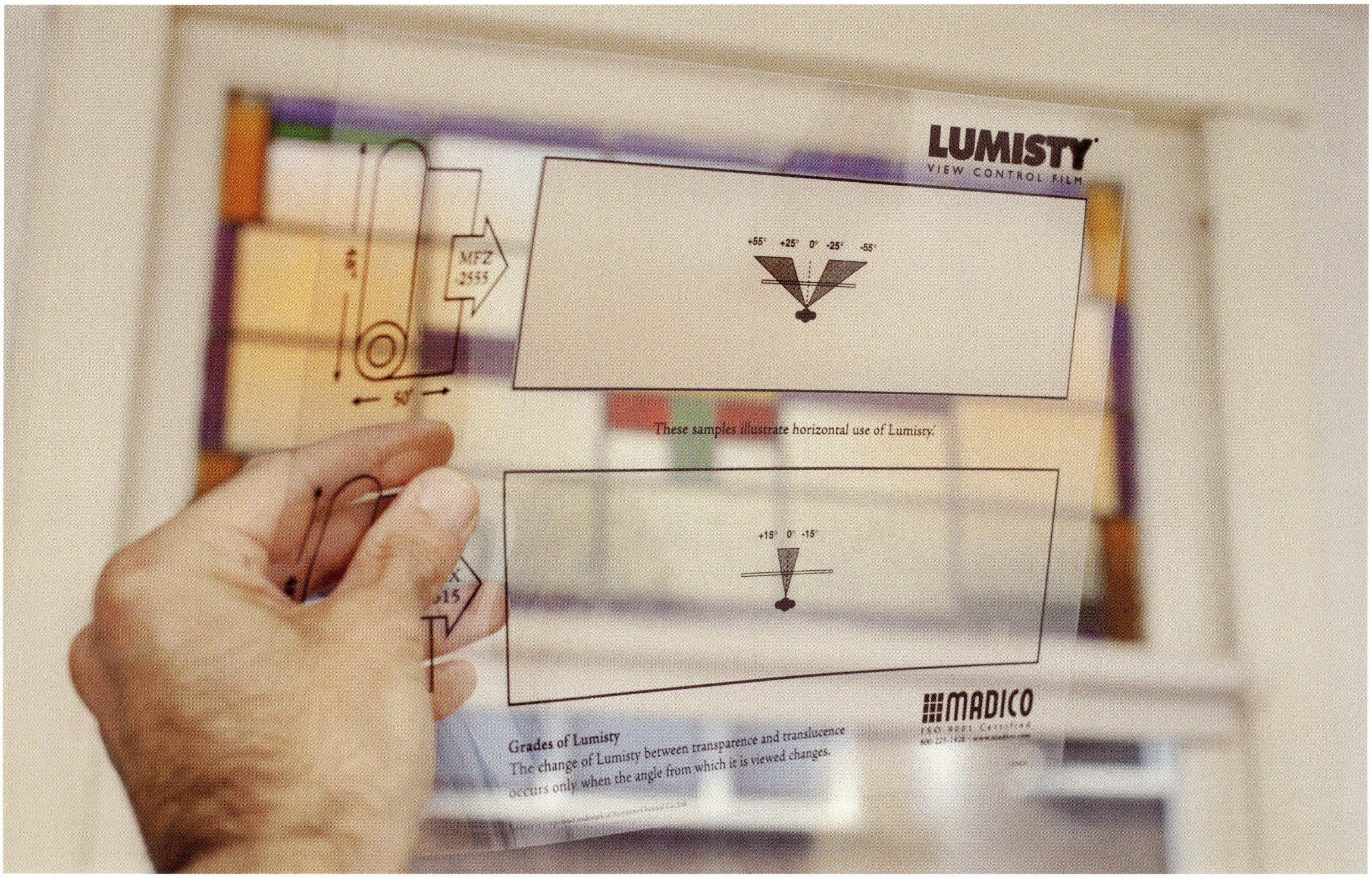
LUMISTY
VIEW CONTROL FILM
MFZ
-2555
50'
+55° +25° 0° -25° -55°
These samples illustrate horizontal use of Lumisty.
+15° 0° -15°
MADICO
ISO 9001 Certified
Grades of Lumisty
The change of Lumisty between transparence and translucence occurs only when the angle from which it is viewed changes.

29

VIEW-CONTROL FILM

Composition
Polyethylene terephthalate (PET)

Properties
Adhesive (easily applied and removed), thin (0.2 to 0.4 mm), alternately translucent and transparent, reflects UV light, suitable for use on various surfaces (glass, acrylic, polycarbonate), functions as a safety film when glass is broken

Applications
Glazed surfaces (windows, partitions, display cases), LCD and computer screens

Contact
Madico
64 Industrial Parkway
Woburn MA 01801
USA
T +1 781 935 7850
F +1 781 935 6841
amurphy@madico.com
www.madico.com

Lintec
23-23 Honcho, Itabashi-ku
Tokyo 173-0001
Japan
T +81 (0)3 5248 7711
pub@lintec.co.jp
www.lintec.co.jp

Photo
The view-control film marketed as Lumisty is either transparent or translucent, depending on the viewing angle.

Lumisty is a view-control film capable of modifying visual possibilities.
It either reflects light or lets it pass through, depending on the angle of incidence. The transformation from transparency to translucence (or vice versa) occurs only when the viewing angle changes. Lumisty is available in three types. MFZ-2555, the bi-angular type, is characterised by double lateral invisibility. The two mono-angular types, MFY-2555 and MFX-1515, are translucent between +25° and +55° and between -15° and +15°, respectively. All three can be used both vertically and horizontally; different orientations create different optical effects. Available on rolls, the material is 1.25 m wide and 15 m long.
View-control film has interesting architectural applications thanks to the dynamic experienced by passers-by. When the film is applied to display windows, the surface may be translucent when viewed frontally, for example, only to become transparent when seen from a more oblique angle. When used on LCD screens, the film bends light emitted by the screen to increase the optical angle, while maintaining the quality of the frontal image. The film was initially developed as a privacy-protection filter for computer screens. Architectural and decorative applications came later.

30

HOLO-GRAPHIC PROJECTION SCREEN

Composition
Laminate of Makrolon sheets and processed film with diffraction mesh

Properties
Transparent or with holographic projection, captivating brilliance, lightweight, strong

Applications
Display windows, exhibitions, trade fairs, showrooms, shops, events and conferences

Technical specifications
PDF downloads via www.holopro.com

Contact
G+B pronova
Lustheide 85
D-51427 Bergisch-Gladbach
Germany
T +49 (0)2204 204 305
F +49 (0)2204 204 300
contact@gb-pronova.de
www.holopro.com

Makroform
Dolivostrasse
D-64293 Darmstadt
Germany
T +49 (0)6151 183 9000
F +49 (0)6151 183 9007
sales@makroform.com
www.makroform.com

Photo
This projection unit features a holographic, transparent screen known as HoloPro.

HoloPro is a transparent projection surface for rear projections, which can be used independently of the ambient light. The screen consists of a specially prepared film laminated between two sheets of Makrolon.
A laser technique is used to create the diffraction mesh on the film, which is then chemically fixed. Diffraction of light on the film produces a holographic image. The image is projected onto the screen from behind, at a calculated angle, and aimed at the viewer by means of holographic-optical elements (HOE). Light passing through the screen from other directions does not interfere with the projection. When nothing is projected onto the surface, HoloPro has the transparency of clear glass. The Makrolon sheets keep the film flat and protect it from environmental influences. Manufactured by Makroform, these synthetic sheets are strong, impact-resistant and lighter than glass.
Compared with other projection surfaces, HoloPro screens have an eye-catching brilliance. The viewer can alternate between looking at the surface and looking through it, and between projected images and a selected background. Because surrounding light striking the HoloPro screen from other angles has almost no effect on the picture quality, the product can be used indoors and out.
The transparency of HoloPro eliminates the physical separation of projection and recording. A camera installed behind a HoloPro screen can make videos of people and activities positioned on the opposite side, while video images recorded elsewhere are simultaneously projected on the same screen.
Participants in a video conference, for example, look one other in the eye and have the feeling of being directly opposite one another.
HoloPro comes in eight standard sizes ranging from 50.8 to 254 cm; film thickness is 180 μ.

31

DOTTED PERSPEX

Composition
Acrylic resin

Properties
Even light emission, optical clarity, durable, recyclable, low energy consumption, low heat generation, re- duced heat-extraction costs, eliminates hot spots

Applications
Retail signage, displays, bus shelters, window ads, shelf and surface illumination, other lighting

Contact
Ineos Acrylics
PO Box 34
Darwen
Lancashire BB3 1QB
UK
T +44 (0)125 487 4000
F +44 (0)125 487 3300
perspex_online@ineos-a.com
acrysales@ineos-a.com
www.perspex.co.uk

Schreinemacher Kunststoffen
Gesworenhoekseweg 10
NL-5047 TM Tilburg
The Netherlands
T +31 (0)13 572 9680
F +31 (0)13 572 9689
kunststoffen@schreinemacher.nl
www.schreinemacher.nl

Photo
Prismex is the name given to panels of Perspex featuring a dot matrix; lighting can be installed at the edges of the panels.

Prismex was created by printing a patented dot matrix onto sheets of clear, poured Perspex. The material was developed for applications requiring peripheral illumination. The dots provide an even distribution of light that is free of the banding effect of conventional backlit signs. In display design, a light source positioned at the edge of a panel rather than behind it makes it possible to build lighter, slimmer constructions. And because the material requires the use of fewer and smaller lamps, Prismex units are more energy efficient and therefore more cost effective.
Though illuminated panel edges do not need flame polishing, they should be router cut or carefully sawed for optimum performance. Non-illuminated edges should be masked.
A gap of 1 to 3 mm between light source and panel edge is essential. Prismex can be both moulded and bent into curved forms.
Prismex has countless applications. Logos and brand names benefit from the clear, sharp image created by the material. A number of companies are currently marketing sign systems that incorporate the Prismex technology. New are applications in which high-output LEDs are inserted along the bottom edge of Prismex panels. The material comes in sheets of 305 x 203 cm and in thicknesses of 5, 10, 12, 15 and 20 mm – a range of options that facilitates prototyping. The textured surface of the sheet minimises handling marks.

32

FLUORES-CENT GLASS TILES

Composition
Glass, luminous pigment

Properties
Weather-resistant, two-dimensional pattern during the day, three-dimensional effect in the dark

Applications
Interior wall decoration (bathrooms, kitchens, pools), architectural glazing (façades, windows, doors, partitions)

Contact
Schott Desag
Hattenbergstrasse 10
D-55122 Mainz
Germany
T +49 (0)6131 66-36 62
F +49 (0)6131 66-40 11
klaus.hofmann@schott.com
www.schott.com

Tapetenfabrik Gebr. Rasch
Raschplatz 1
49565 Bramsche
Germany
T +49 (0)5461 810
F +49 (0)5461 811 15
info@rasch.de
www.rasch.de

RC Tritec
Speicherstrasse
CH-9053 Teufen
Switzerland
T +41 (0)71 335 7373
F +41 (0)71 335 7374
sales@rctritec.com
www.rctritec.com

Photo
Shown are prototypes of Onda, a glass tile, and Linea and Corso, wallpaper patterns, by night and by day (design: Gruppe Re).

Fluorescent glass tiles are manufactured using the printing process normally applied to façade panelling. Three layers of glass enamel are printed in sequence on the back of float glass and then burnt onto the surface of the tile at a firing temperature between 650° and 720°C for two to four minutes. Unique is the use of luminous pigment in ceramic enamel, giving unprecedented chromatic depth and durability to a pattern that changes according to the amount of light available. The pigment collects UV rays (from natural or artificial light) that produce a bright greenish-yellow light in the dark (the effect lasts about an hour). The luminous substance is combined with two additional background colours: red or turquoise.
Another use of luminous pigments is seen in Gruppe RE's wallpaper designs (Linea and Corso). Here the pigment is layered with other colours, through which the design shines with varying intensities of greenish-yellow, creating a three-dimensional impression in the dark. Both wallpaper and glass tiles are prototypes intended for series production.

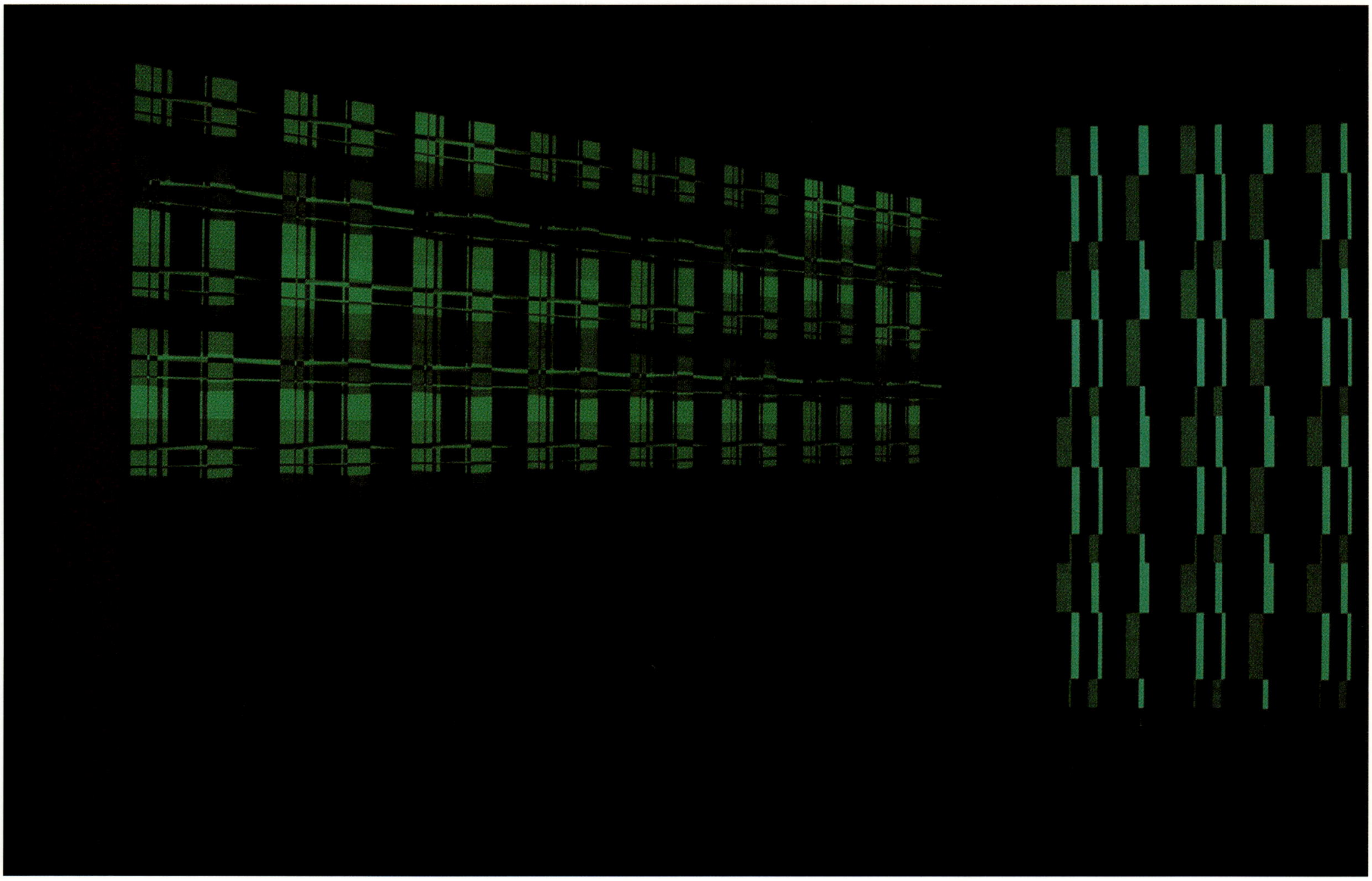

33

ILLUSIVE FILM

Composition
Vinyl or polycarbonate

Properties
Translucent, illusive, flexible

Applications
Graphics, flooring, wall coverings, fixtures

Technical specifications
www.e-iosk.com

Contact
Creative Environments
4930 SW 29th Ave.
Dania FL 33312
USA
T +1 954 983 2755
F +1 954 983 2017
ken@illusionflex.com
www.e-iosk.com
www.illusionflex.com

Photo
Illusion Flex is a thin vinyl or polycarbonate film containing thousands of optical lenses that combine with a graphic pattern to create illusive, 3-D effects.

Illusion Flex is a 0.038-cm-thick vinyl or polycarbonate film containing thousands of strategically positioned optical lenses. These reflective lenses work in combination with one of several standard patterns to produce not simply a 3-D effect, but an illusion. The swirling illusions include fire, flowing water, ice and molten metal. The positioning of the lenses and the selected pattern combine to create the illusion. Various lighting effects, particularly those achieved by backlighting, bring the film to life. Daylight results in a less dramatic illusion than that created by some type of artificial reflective lighting.
The product can be cold-formed, diecut and heat-sealed. Printing methods for Illusion Flex include silk screeing, ink jet and vinyl transfer. The hallucinative film can be bonded to surfaces ranging from wood, drywall, plywood and plaster to MDF, plastics, metals and fibreglass. Available are 21 colours, as well as 4 vinyl and 3 polycarbonate patterns. Illusion Flex comes on rolls 60.96 cm wide and 76.2 or 152.4 m in length.
There are numerous applications. A marine retailer is using Illusion Flex as a window cling to create the illusion of flowing water on storefront windows. It is also being used to mimic condensation in a beer-bottle display. The material is highly suitable for cladding walls, columns and other vertical surfaces in public venues like restaurants, cinemas and nightclubs. Creative Environments is currently setting up a fashion line that features Illusion Flex.

34

INTER-LAYER FOR LAMINATED GLASS

Composition
Polyvinyl butyral (PVB), heat- and light-stable pigments

Properties
Similar to laminated glass in terms of safety, sound control and solar-energy control; available in different colours and designs

Applications
Architectural glazing (interior and exterior), retail display, automotive industry

Contact
Solutia
575 Maryville Centre Drive
St Louis MO 63131
USA
vanceva.solutions@solutia.com
www.vanceva.com

Photo
Special interlayers add colour to laminated glass at Miami Airport's Harmonic Runway.

Plastic interlayers strengthen laminated glass. And special interlayers used to create coloured and patterned glass provide architects and designers with virtually unlimited options in this area. Vanceva Design features a tough protective interlayer known as polyvinyl butyral (PVB), the high-performance component in laminated glass. When heat and pressure are used to bond a PVB-based interlayer between two or more panes of glass, the result is durable, adaptable, shatter-resistant glazing that reduces the risk of injury and property damage. In terms of aesthetics, the product can be used, for example, to create a kaleidoscopic wall of clear and coloured glass. Available patterns include dots, squares, bands, weave and cross. Another interlayer, Vanceva Color, is made with heat- and light-stable pigments for an intense, long-lasting chromatic effect. The system consists of eight transparent, coloured PVB interlayers that can be used alone or combined (four layers maximum) to produce more than 600 translucent colours. The chromatic interlayer system can be used in combination with tinted glass and/or reflective coatings to create even more colours.
Used together, Vanceva Design and Vanceva Color offer a wide range of design solutions.

35

TILED LIGHT WALL

Composition
Ceramic tiles, fluorescent lighting, wood or aluminium framework

Properties
Custom-made, interactive, modular, suitable for all 15-x-15 cm tiles, all colours of light possible

Applications
Hotels, restaurants, bars, shops, offices, public spaces, waiting rooms, lounges

Contact
Rogier Sterk
Apeldoornsestraat 14
NL-6828 AB Arnhem
The Netherlands
T +31 (0)26 445 1600
r.sterk@tiscali.nl

Photo
The tiled light wall offers architects and designers an opportunity to play with light.

Designer Rogier Sterk's 'tiled light wall' consists of basic ceramic tiles on an illuminated background. Each tile is attached to a mechanism that allows it to be pressed and released. A tile left untouched appears to be lit only around the edges. Press a tile and the underlying light shines across its surface, emitting a reflection.
The system requires a standard light switch that regulates the lighting, which is not activated by pressing a tile. Switched on, a wall of untouched tiles continues to emit light through the joints between tiles. The amount of light is determined by the position of the tiles.
The press-release mechanisms work best when a blind wall is installed 30 cm in front of an existing wall. The system also requires a framework that contains both blind wall and mechanisms. The larger the surface area, the greater the opportunity to create complex and varied patterns of light. A modular product like this one imposes no limitations on surface area. Standard tiles (15 x 15 cm) of any colour are suitable. Countless designs can be created by combining various colours (including white) of tile and light.
The tiled light wall is ideal for public spaces. It is an eye-catching element that makes people aware of, and invites them to interact with, their surroundings. It can reinforce the identity of a building or highlight a corporate logo.

36

HIGH-REFLECTANCE METAL

Composition
Aluminium or steel substrate, metallised polyester film, adhesive

Properties
Total reflectance of 97 per cent, mirror-like appearance, durable, easy to clean, no forming restrictions, no crazing on bends, non-iridescent

Applications
Lighting products, architectural elements, displays, reflectors and other products requiring high reflectance

Technical specifications
Downloads via www.laminatesandcomposites.com

Contact
MSC Laminates and Composites
2300 East Pratt Blvd.
Elk Grove Village IL 60007-5995
USA
T +1 847 439 1822
F +1 847 806 2219
www.laminatesandcomposites.com

Photo
Specular+ is a highly reflective material (97 per cent reflectance) with a substrate of steel or aluminium.

Specular+ is a high-reflectance material for fluorescent light fixtures and reflectors; it is a viable alternative to anodised aluminium.
Manufacturing begins with Magnetron Sputtered Vacuum Deposition (MSVD), a metallising process that deposits a layer of pure silver onto a clear, 0.0025-cm-thick polyester film. The second step is a continuous coil-coating process that chemically bonds the film to wide coils of metal. The process involves a thermoset, cross-linked system. The result is a film-tearing bond strength that prevents delamination.
The material is manufactured in coil form on a substrate of steel or aluminium. It is sold in coil and cut sheet or in blank form. Available are thicknesses from 0.4 to 0.8 mm, widths up to 122.5 cm and various lengths.

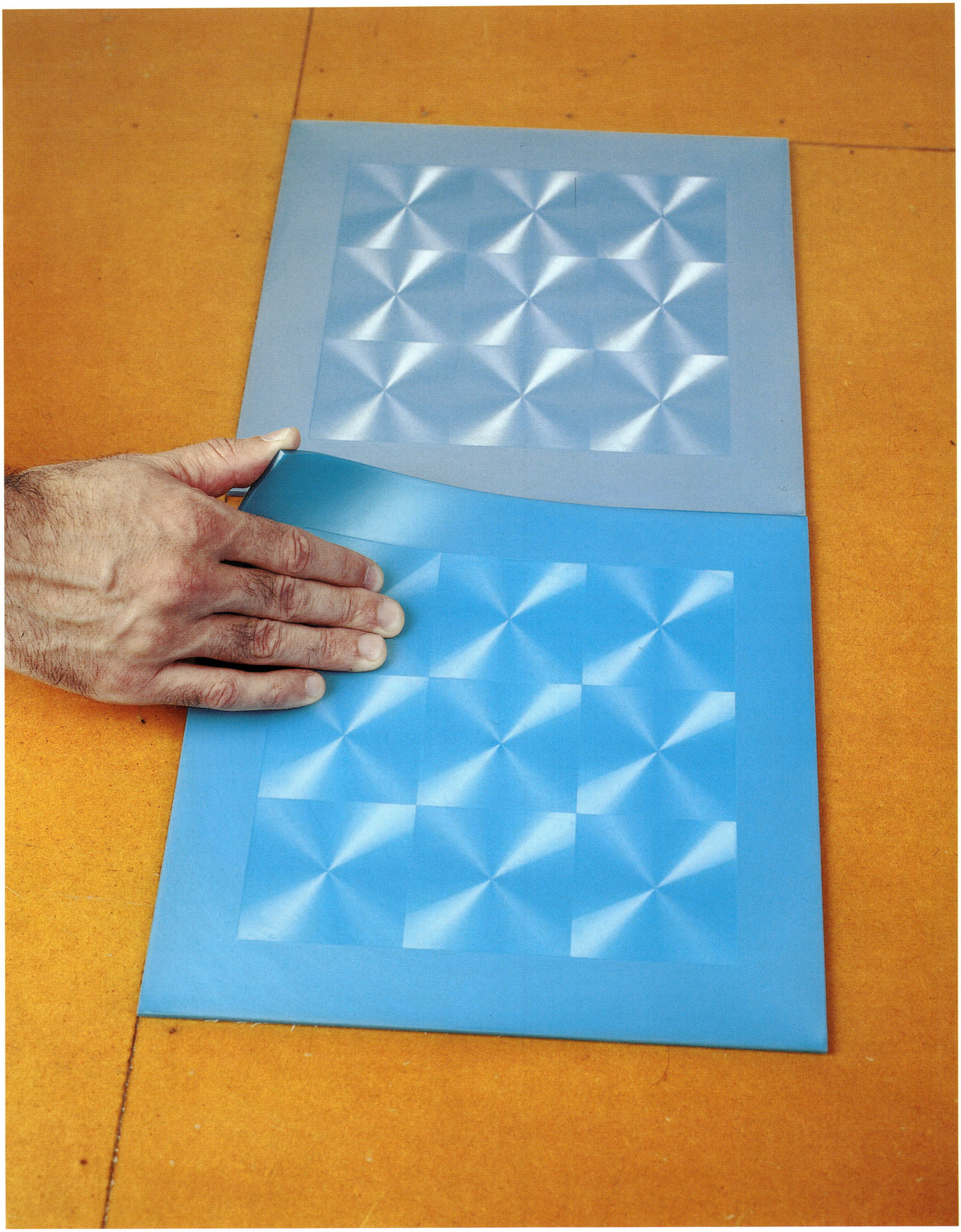

37

SOFT TILE

Composition
Polyurethane, pearlised pigments

Properties
Looks solid, feels soft, transparent, flexible, elastic, durable, non-corrosive

Applications
Walls, floors

Contact
Saar Oosterhof
Albrachthof 25
NL-3581 WV Utrecht
The Netherlands
T +31 (0)30 658 6557
F +31 (0)30 658 6556
vormgever@saar.nl
www.saar.nl

Photo
Prototype of Saar Oosterhof's soft tile.

Designer Saar Oosterhof experiments with soft, transparent, rubbery materials like polyurethane and silicone. Her surprising creations feel immediately soft to the touch. A good example is Oosterhof's soft tiles of hand-cast polyurethane combined with glitter. When applied, the hologram structures give floor or wall an illusion of depth; the image changes with the incidence of light and the viewing angle. Experimental prototypes of these flexible tiles feature varying structures, surface textures and colours. The product now being manufactured, Lens Tile, has undergone a few changes, the most important being the use of pearlised pigments instead of glitter. Lens Tile, which creates an iridescent effect, relies on injection-moulding technology.

38

CHROMATIC FABRICS

Composition
Polyurethane face, double-knit polyester backing

Properties
Colour-shifting effects, diverse fabrics possible

Applications
Upholstery, wall coverings, footwear, apparel

Contact
Sommers Plastic Products
81 Kuller Road
Clifton NJ 07015
USA
T +1 973 777 7888
F +1 973 345 1586
sales@sommers.com
www.sommers.com

Flex Products
1402 Mariner Way
Santa Rosa CA 95407-7370
USA
T +1 707 525 7007
F +1 707 525 7537
chromaflair@flexprod.com

Photo
Chromatic fabrics contain light-interference pigments that create bright, highly saturated colours which shift with the viewing angle, as well as the light source.

Chromatic fabrics contain light-interference pigments incorporated into cast polyurethane resin and laminated onto circular-knit polyester fabrics. The light-interference pigments are based on a patented pigment developed by the aerospace industry and manufactured by Flex Products. The pigment creates bright, highly saturated colours that shift with the viewing angle, as well as the light source. Sommers Plastic has captured the dramatic iridescence of butterfly wings, the metallic lustre of semiprecious minerals and the pearly radiance of seashells and incorporated these effects into a durable high-tech textile. The fabrics pass all specifications for contract furnishings, such as fire rating, abrasion resistance, colourfastness and tear strength.
The 137-cm-wide fabrics are available in various patterns and in more than 20 colours. They can be used for upholstery, wall coverings, athletic footwear (certain Nike models, for example) and apparel. DesignTex distributes the products to the contract-architecture and design trade under the name Presto Change-O.

77% POLYURETHANE • 23% POLYESTER

54" WIDE/137 CM • PUT UP: 60 YARD ROLLS/55 MTRS

LEUCITE
PYRITE
MARCASITE
ALMANDINE
BARITE
MALACHITE
TOURMALINE
PERIDOT
AZURITE
LAZULITE
MUSCOVITE

QUARTZ
JASPER
MICA
AMETHYST
CITRON
GARNET
CARNELIAN
GOLD
TOPAZ
NICKEL

FLE
XIBL
EST
RUC
TUR
ES

INTRO

Intensive experimentation with flexible structures has been around since the sixties, an era in which Frei Otto, studying the possibilities of tensile tent structures, solved the problem of stress concentration. Close relatives of Otto's tensile structures are the inflatables: large air-filled walls used for mobile exhibitions and temporary pavilions. Walter Neumark experimented with inflatables in the sixties. A well-known example featured at Expo 70 in Osaka was the Fuji Pavilion, a high-pressure, tensile, tubular structure.

The futuristic research of yesteryear has reached commercial maturity. Today's tensioned membranes and stretch ceilings are exceedingly versatile and highly durable. They withstand extreme climatic conditions and have low maintenance requirements. Fascinating applications of these materials include the Millennium Dome in London and a German airship hangar called the CargoLifter, both built by Birdair.

Inflatable structures have also become big business. Braun Wagner manufactures reusable inflatable stands that can be erected in minutes. Another interesting example is Basic House, a design by the Spaniard Martín Ruiz de Azúa. His 'dwelling' is made of double-sided metallised polyester of the sort normally used as insulating material for weather balloons and satellites.

A wearable building inflated by body heat or sunlight, Basic House was conceived as a shelter for illegal immigrants. It protects the user from both heat and cold. Extremely light and thin, it can be folded up and carried in a pocket.

Ideas like these take forty-year-old experiments with flexible structures and lift them to a higher level.

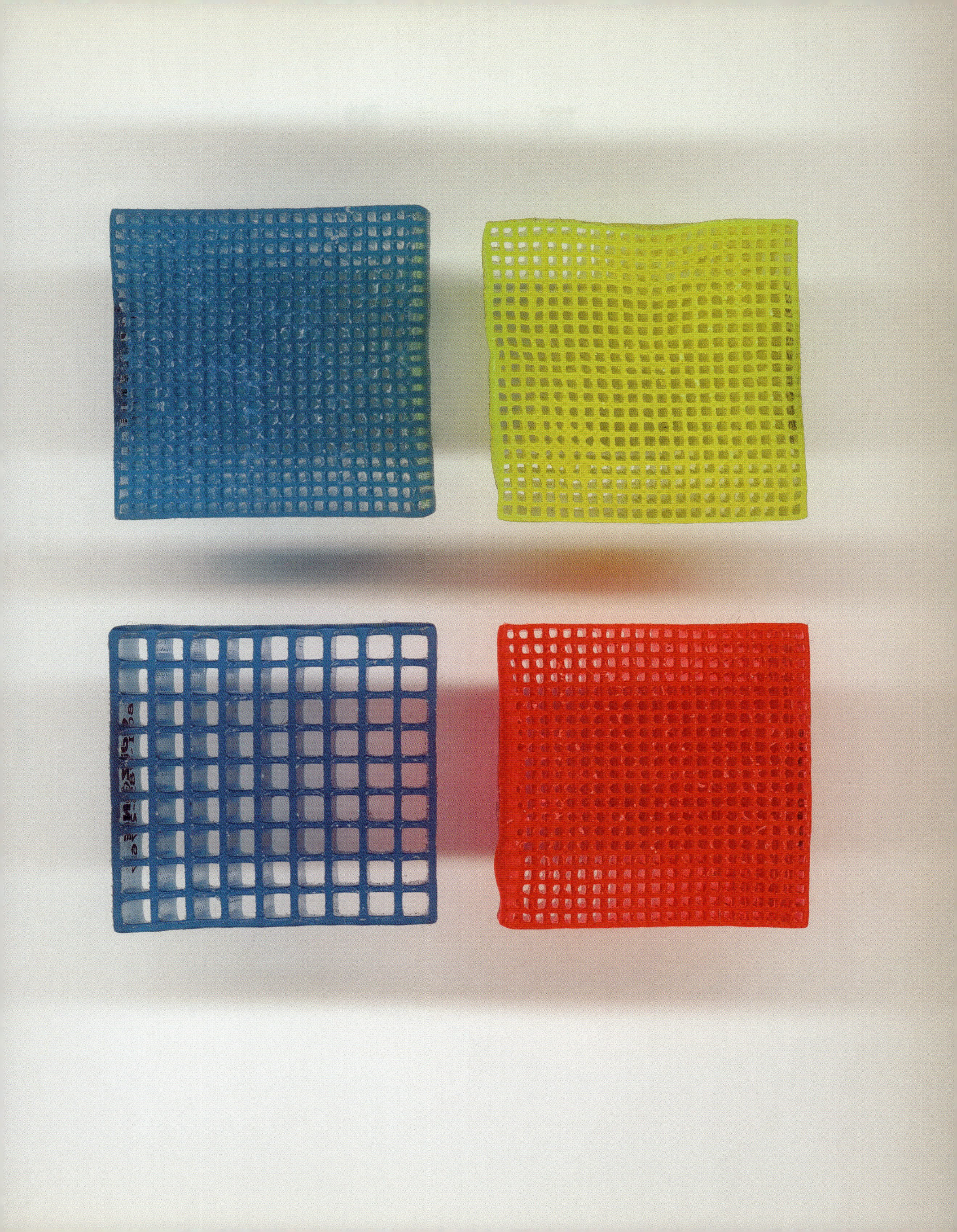

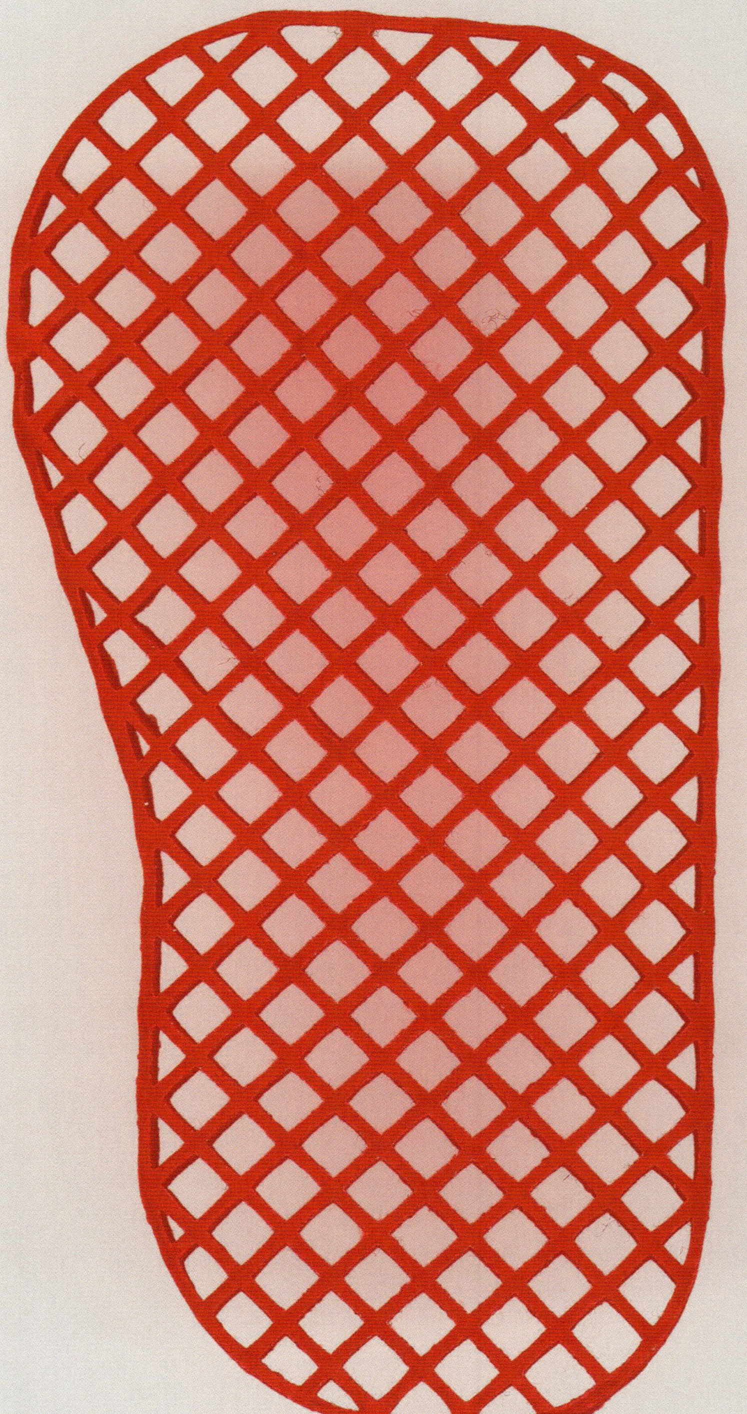

39

INTELLIGENT GEL FOAM

Composition
Copolymer, elastomer

Properties
Strong, durable, shock-absorbent, heat-resistant, hypoallergenic, non-toxic, tactile (has a soft, rubbery feel), equalises pressure, reduces vibration

Applications
Mattresses, cushions, footwear

Contact
EdiZone LC
220 North 1300 West #1
Pleasant Grove UT 84062
USA
T +1 801 785 2767
F +1 801 785 2611
joe@edizone.com
www.edizone.com

Photo
Available in fluorescent colours, Intelli-Gel consists of a grid of hollow tubes that remain erect under lighter loads, but buckle when a certain degree of pressure is applied.

Intelli-Gel is short for Intelligent Gelastic Foam, a soft-but-strong elastomeric material composed of a grid of hollow tubes designed to support lighter loads and to buckle when a certain degree of pressure is applied. The result is equal support and equal pressure at all points of contact. When the gel is stretched to over ten times its resting length and then released, it snaps back into shape instantly. The durable material is an excellent alternative for foam or solidified gel.
Because Intelli-Gel's elastomeric formula can be modified, as can the dimensions of the tubular cells and their walls, countless varieties are possible. Cell shapes include square, rectangular, triangular and circular. Since tubes are generally positioned perpendicular to the cushioned load, the material is suitable for products of virtually any size and application. Intelli-Gel does not come in rolls or sheets. The water-clear gel can be coloured or otherwise treated to create a translucent, pastel and/or fluorescent look, among others.

40

POWER-STRETCH FABRIC

Composition
Elastic monofilaments

Properties
Elastic, keeps its shape (even after rigorous stretching), has an open structure, prevents accumulation of heat and moisture

Applications
Seating, clothing, footwear

Contact
Schoeller Textil
Bahnhofstrasse 17
CH-9475 Sevelen
Switzerland
T +41 (0)81 786 0800
F +41 (0)81 786 0810
info@schoeller-textiles.com
www.schoeller-textiles.com

Photo
Dynatec is an open-structured, elastic fabric that breathes.

A dynamic material with an open, transparent look and a high degree of elasticity is a good description of Schoeller Textil's Dynatec. The fabric keeps its shape even after rigorous stretching thanks to elastic monofilaments, which combine ergonomically efficient elasticity with high stability and transparency. The benefits are particularly apparent when the material is used as a seat covering: the user practically sits in the fabric, which does not sag or lose its shape. The fabric is stretched across a frame that needs no extra cushioning, upholstery or support. There is no accumulation of heat or moisture. The Dynatec range includes a light, gauzy design and heavier options suitable for seating and footwear.

41

LAMINATED SAILCLOTH

Composition
Polyester, other synthetic fibres (Kevlar, Technora, Spectra, Dyneema, Vectran), nonwoven carbon inserts, dyed adhesives

Properties
Strong, lightweight, semitransparent, durable, low-stretch, high UV stability

Applications
Genoas, mainsails, front-end materials

Contact
Dimension-Polyant
Speefeld 7
D-47906 Kempen
Germany
T +49 (0)2152 891 0
F +49 (0)2152 891 149
info@dimension-polyant.com
www.dimension-polyant.com

Photo
X-Ply sailcloth is a durable composite fabric with a high strength/weight ratio.

X-Ply is the brand name of a fabric with off-the-warp support. The fabric is made by inserting continuous strands of yarn at various angles of the warp in an X-shaped pattern. The resulting product is stronger and more durable than traditional sailcloth, but also heavier and more expensive. Various combinations of synthetic fibres and colours form the basis of a wide range of attractive options, including fabrics with a distinctive look and/or colour, as well as sailcloth suitable for specific functions.

42

FIBREGLASS TEXTILE

Composition
Fibreglass, synthetic resin

Properties
High strength/weight ratio, suitable for three-dimensional forms (such as cylinders), excellent mechanical qualities, simple to use, insulating, translucent (in combination with certain resins), easy to repair, can be impregnated in open mould or applied directly to backing, drapable

Applications
Architecture and building (cladding, exhibition panels, billboards, amusement parks, radar domes, factory ceilings), transport (boats, hardtops, nose cones and interior panels of trains, trailers/caravans), niche products (portable showers, flight cases)

Contact
Parabeam 3D Glass Fabrics
PO Box 134
NL-5700 AC Helmond
The Netherlands
T +31 (0)492 570 625
F +31 (0)492 570 733
sales@parabeam.nl
www.parabeam3d.com

Photo
Parabeam, a three-dimensional fibreglass textile, consists of two woven outer layers connected by upright fibreglass pile yarns. Illustrated are an impregnated and a non-impregnated example of the material.

Parabeam, a three-dimensional fibreglass textile, has a sandwich structure consisting of two woven outer layers connected by upright fibreglass pile yarns woven directly into these layers. Different weaving techniques produce different thicknesses (3 to 22 mm). The material has its origins in the manufacture of velour, a fabric whose cut pile exposes a tactile structure of upright tufts of yarn.
When the material is impregnated with epoxy, polyester or vinylester, the pile springs up automatically and uniformly – thanks to the capillary effect of the fibreglass – to the predetermined height. The result of this quick, easy process is a strong, lightweight sandwich material capable of replacing the standard sandwich panels and solid laminates (woods, foams, honeycombs) used for walls, floors and ceilings. The hollow space between the two outer layers, which makes the material a good insulator, allows gases and fluids to pass through. Panels made of the impregnated material can be clad in stone, wood, HPL or aluminium.
Application of a plastic film produces a smoother surface. Parabeam can be foamed to in-crease mechanical properties and/or to seal the hollow space between the outer layers.

43

METAL WEAVES

Composition
Stainless steel, carbon, bronze, combinations of metal and synthetics, special materials (Monel metal, Hastelloy, Inconel, titanium and so forth)

Properties
Flexible or rigid (depending on the material), transparent to nearly opaque, scratchproof, contributes to good acoustics

Applications
Process belts, filtration and separation equipment, shielding devices, architecture and interior design (walls, ceilings, floors)

Contact
GDK
Metallweberstrasse 46
D-52348 Duren
Germany
info@gdk.de
www.gdk.de

Photo
Pictured is a full-scale sample of a plain weave.

Metal weaves, once used primarily for technical applications, are now valued by architects and designers for their reflective qualities and interesting surface effects. A metal-weave mesh that appears rather transparent from one angle can look almost opaque when viewed from another perspective. Layering a number of meshes creates a moiré effect. The material comes in various thicknesses. Specially designed weaves can be shaped to move in both directions like a sail. Because metal weaves are a good acoustical material, architects can use them in the interiors of opera houses, concert halls and other public buildings. Because they are scratch-resistant, they make good coverings for the walls of easily vandalised areas like lifts. Certain types are suitable as flooring; GDK's Tatami, for example, is abrasion-resistant, durable and easy to clean. Other applications include projection surfaces and ceilings for trade-fair stands.
Clad in stainless-steel Escale mesh, a project-specific material, Bertelsmann Planet-M (Expo 2000, Hannover) glistened throughout the day in its coat of reflected natural light. At night, when the surface of Planet-M was illuminated by 380 lamps, the filigreed surface functioned as a diffuser of light.
Dominique Perrault used Sambesi, a stainless-steel fabric with a 40-percent open mesh, to clad the vaulted ceiling of the Bibliothèque Nationale de France in Paris.

44

FLEXIBLE ADHESIVE STRIP

Composition
Polypropylene, resin-modified acrylic glue

Properties
Easy to apply, dries instantly, unaffected by casters, cleanable, tolerates temperatures from -20° to +50°C during transport/storage and temperatures to +30°C when in use, unsuitable for heated floors and outdoor use

Applications
Quick installation of fibre- or felt-backed floor covering (interior design, stand design, trade fairs, museums)

Contact
Henkel Bautechnik
PO Box 10 28 52
D-40019 Dusseldorf
Germany
T +49 (0)211 73 790
F +49 (0)211 73 79-290
thomsit@henkel.de
www.henkel.com

Photo
Thomsit T 2000 High-Tack is an adhesive strip used to attach floor coverings. Applying the strip is a one-step operation, after which the floor covering can be removed when desired and a new one installed, time and again.

The Thomsit High-Tack system, which consists of polypropylene and resin-modified acrylic glue and boasts 3 million micro tack points per square metre, is used to attach floor coverings. When a strip is applied to the backing of a fibre- or felt-backed floor covering, these tack points fasten the covering securely, even in the case of wall-to-wall carpeting. The product is a good alternative for carpet glue; it can be used on a levelled foundation, an elevated modular floor, a chipboard subfloor or an existing floor that has been well cleaned. Installation of wall-to-wall carpeting in the home requires application of an adhesive strip only to the edges of the carpet.
Thomsit High-Tack is a costs-reducing solution for public spaces that endure intensive pedestrian traffic. The product is also suitable for venues with flooring that changes frequently, such as exhibition spaces, museums, restaurants and trade-fair stands. It facilitates the addition, modification or replacement of designs and patterns. Thomsit High-Tack is a one-step operation that allows for later renovation free of demolition costs and the need for levelling or preparing the surface in any way. A simple exchange of old flooring for new means less refuse and thus less strain on the environment.

45

METALLISED PLASTIC FILM

Composition
Double-sided metallised polyester, PET or polyimide (Kapton)

Properties
Lightweight, reflective, foldable, strong, thin, protects against heat and cold

Applications
Protection and thermal insulation (communication satellites, weather balloons, aeroplanes, cryogenics, motors, rescue blankets)

Technical specifications
www.aerospace-technology.com/contractors/thermal/trico (among others)

Contact
DuPont Teijin Films US
Barley Mill Plaza, Bldg. 27
Lancaster Pike & Route 141
P.O. Box 80027
Wilmington DE 19880-0027
USA
T +1 804 530 9339
F +1 804 530 9867
www.dupontteijinfilms.com
www.dupont.com/kapton

Tricon
Hausenerweg 1
D-79111 Freiburg
Germany
T +49 (0)761 490 46-0
F +49 (0)761 490 46-79
scherzinger@tricon-gmbh.de
www.tricon-gmbh.de

Martín Ruiz de Azúa
Aribau 230 8°
E-08006 Barcelona
Spain
T/F +34 (0)93 414 6582
mrazua@teleline.es

Photo
Prototype of Martín Ruiz de Azúa's Basic House, a reversible shelter of metallised film that protects the wearer from heat and cold.

Few other products composed of so little material provide the level of protection and insulation derived from metallised plastic film. Because of its thermal and optical properties, the film is used for insulating satellites and motors and for making rescue blankets. It can be found in the equipment required for desert, polar and mountain-climbing expeditions. Metallised plastic film is a standard insulating material for aeroplanes. It is used in cryogenics. The outermost layer of the film provides a reflective surface for radio signals. The type normally used for thermal insulation is made of PET or polyimide (Kapton). Cryogenic use requires PET film. Kapton tolerates high temperatures (up to 350°C). After coating the film with a layer of metal, companies like Tricon varnish or laminate the metallised result. Spanish designer Martín Ruiz de Azúa uses the film in a different context. He created Basic House – a small, reversible structure inflated by body heat or sunlight – as a shelter for illegal immigrants. Extremely light (200 g) and thin (13 microns), it can be folded up and carried in a pocket. It reverses to protect the wearer from either heat or cold. The shiny gold side reflects 90 per cent of the sun's rays; worn with the gold side out, Basic House ventilates the body. The silver side keeps the user dry and warm, while maintaining body temperature.

46

WOVEN HEATING TEXTILES

Composition
Stainless steel, copper, acrylic adhesives, glass yarn, polypropylene yarn, polyester yarn, copper/PVC or copper/silicone wiring

Properties
Flexible, heats quickly (operating temperature of 80°C), has a folding resistance of more than 2000 folds, can be pleated

Applications
Medical sector, automotive and transport industries, building industry, bedding, agriculture

Contact
Textiles y Energia Enertex
Mare De Deu Del Pilar St. Andreu De Llavaneres
E-08392 Barcelona
Spain
T +34 (0)6 6978 5112
F +34 (0)93 792 9183
enertex@inicia.es

Photo
Pictured is a woven heating textile made of polypropylene/polyester yarn and stainless steel.

This electrically heated textile is thin, durable and highly suitable for industrial applications. Woven heating textiles are composed of stainless steel, copper film, acrylic adhesives, glass yarn, polypropylene yarn, polyester yarn, and copper/PVC or copper/silicone connecting wiring. The textiles have integral, flexible connections and are designed to operate on a power source not exceeding 50V. The product can be custom designed to almost any size. The minimum order is 200 pieces. Machine-washable versions are available. As the heat transmission is mainly by radiation, the surface must be black, but in some cases the heating element can be given a more colourful covering. Heating textiles can be used in combination with foams impregnated with phase-changing materials. Applications include rescue mattresses, life jackets, car seats, geo textiles, robot housing, radar-detection garments and external heating elements for the insulation of water tanks. The product is not CE-approved for domestic use. The way in which the polypropylene and polyester yarn is combined with stainless- steel wire produces a material that can be pleated, which makes it suitable for other purposes as well.

47

SCULPTURAL ALUMINIUM SHEETS

Composition
Formed aluminium (alloy #3003)

Properties
Lightweight, folds longitudinally, lets light and sound pass through (when perforated), has mat silver finish with UV protection

Applications
Interior and retail design (cladding for ceilings, walls, columns and doors), displays, furniture, lighting, signage, electronic equipment

Technical specifications
Downloads via
www.forms-surfaces.com/
products/aero/index.html

Contact
Surfaces+ (Forms + Surfaces)
6395 Cindy Lane
Carpinteria CA 93013
USA
T +1 877 626 7788
F +1 805 684 8620
marketing@forms-surfaces.com
www.forms-surfaces.com

Fielitz
Brunnhausgasse 3
D-85049 Ingolstadt
Germany
T +49 (0)841 935 140
F +49 (0)841 935 1413
info@fielitz.de
www.fielitz.de

Photo
Aero sculptural anodised-aluminium sheets are flexible and formable. They are a creative resource for use in interior design.

Aero is the brand name of a line of tightly corrugated anodised-aluminium sheet material. The flexible, formable sheets can be rolled like a carpet. Crisp folds cast deep shadows that contribute to the three-dimensional appearance of the material.
Variations in thickness and depth combine with rounded or squared edges to produce a range of creative options. Certain types have precision-engineered perforations, for example, which allow light and sound to permeate the supple folds, giving the material a breathable quality.
Aero is at once high-tech and refined. The material can be used for the geometric compositions and fluid curves so attractive in counter facings and retail displays. It can be rolled as a decorative panel across the ceiling and down the hall to be shaped into seating. It cannot be used as a structural member or to reinforce or brace a structural member.
Aero is available by the case in five different designs. Each case contains 10 to 16 sheets 45 cm wide by 116 cm long. Prefabricated panelled versions of Aero are also available. All products have a mat silver finish.

48

STAINLESS-STEEL SHEER

Composition
Polyester, powdered stainless steel

Properties
Decorative, elastic, has a metallic look

Applications
Interior design (curtains, draperies), fade protection

Contact
Clarence House
3/10 Chelsea Harbour Design Centre
Chelsea Harbour
London SW10 OXE
UK
T +44 (0)20 7351 1200
F +44 (0)20 7351 6300
sales@clarencehouse.co.uk
www.clarencehouse.com

Photo
Stainless-steel sheer is a woven polyester mesh coated with powdered stainless steel.

This completely woven polyester mesh sports a coat of powdered stainless steel that gives it a sheer effect. The fabric, which has a mat side and a shiny side, complies with NFPA 701, a UK National Fire Prevention Agency standard for flame resistance. Applications for stainless-steel sheer include fade protection where environment containment is required.

14-16AWG SES 14-16AWG SES 14-16AWG SES 14-16AWG SES 14-16AWG SES 14-16AWG SES 14-16AWG SES 14-16AWG SES 14-16AWG SES

49

HEAT-SHRINK TUBING

Composition
Polyolefins

Properties
Flexible or semi-rigid, sturdy, insulating, protective, flame-retardant (certain types)

Applications
(depending on type used)
Flame-retardant coverings, protective coatings for wire splices and harness breakouts (automotive and marine industries), insulating/environmental coatings for wiring and electronic components

Contact
National Standard Parts
4400 Mobile Highway
Pensacola FL 32506
USA
T +1 850 874 6813
F +1 850 456 5376
info@nationalstandardparts.com
www.nationalstandardparts.com

Photo
One type of heat-shrink tubing shrinks to 25 per cent of its diameter when heated.

Polyolefin tubing that shrinks when heated between 121° and 135°C provides a protective, insulating coating for wiring and electronic components in different shapes and sizes. Shrink ratio varies from 2:1 to 4:1, depending on the type of tubing. The material is available in a range of lengths, diameters and types. One example is flame-retardant tubing (black only) with an internal layer of thermoplastic adhesive that forms a barrier against contaminants. Thanks to its thin-walled structure, this flexible tubing conforms easily to irregular shapes. It is used as a protective coating for wire splices and harness breakouts in the automotive and marine industries. It can also provide environmental protection for electronic components. One type shrinks to 25 per cent of its diameter when heated; it covers large disparities in underlying material. The heavy-walled HST600 series features a sturdy, semi-rigid tubing suitable for underwater and underground environments.

50

CORRUGATED BOARD

Composition
Pressed cellulose

Properties
Lightweight (1.2 to 2.7 kg/m2), strong, flexible, corrugated, can be treated and used like wood

Applications
Shop fitting, trade-fair stands, furniture

Technical specifications
Downloads via www.well.de/en/wellboard_en.html

Contact
Well Ausstellungssystem
Schwarzer Bär 2
D-30449 Hannover
Germany
T +49 (0)511 92881-10
F +49 (0)511 92881-18
info@well.de
www.well.de

Photo
Made of pressed cellulose, Wellboard is lightweight, strong and flexible.

Wellboard is a corrugated board of hot-pressed cellulose manufactured in a process that requires no adhesives. Remarkably lightweight, strong and flexible, the material is ideal for creating attractive curves and edges. Much like wood, Wellboard can be painted, varnished and glued to other materials.
Five types of Wellboard are available: Minimum, Medium, Maximum, Alpha and Gamma. Three are similar to corrugated board: Minimum (1 mm thick, with a 4.5-mm profile), Medium (2 mm thick, with a profile of 7 mm), and Maximum (1.5 mm thick, with a profile of 8.5 mm).
The 1-mm-thick Alpha has an amplitude of 12 mm; here the corrugated design is not completely rounded. Also 1 mm thick, Gamma has a trapezium profile.
The material can be used to build stands and to make furniture; interior designers can use it as a surface material or to create partitions.

51

SUPER-STRONG FIBRE

Composition
Polyethylene (PE)

Properties
High specific strength, high specific modulus, lightweight (floats on water), low elongation to break, high energy absorption and flex resistance, radar-transparent, melting point between 144° and 155°C, conducts heat well, recyclable, easy to clean, approved for skin contact, resistant to UV light, chemicals, moisture and impact

Applications
Fabrics, clothing, composite reinforcement (rope, nets, bulletproof vests, vehicle armouring, protective clothing, safety doors)

Contact
DSM High Performance Fibers
PO Box 6510
NL-6401 JH Heerlen
The Netherlands
T +31 (0)45 543 6878
F +31 (0)45 543 6800
info.dsmhpf@dsm.com
www.dyneema.com

Photo
Dyneema is a super-strong fibre used, for example, to weave tough, bulletproof fabrics.

Dyneema is an ultra-high-strength, low-density polyethylene fibre. In terms of weight, it is 15 times stronger than steel. It boasts a high degree of energy absorption and excellent resistance to wear, water, UV radiation and chemicals. Polyethylene (PE) was selected for its ultra-high molecular weight, but the non-oriented molecules in standard polyethylene are easily torn apart. Dyneema, on the other hand, undergoes a gel-spinning process in which a solvent dissolves the molecules before extruding them through a spinneret. In the solvent solution, the molecules that form clusters in the solid state become disentangled and remain so. As the fibre is drawn, an extremely high level of macro-molecular orientation is attained, resulting in a fibre with a high tenacity and modulus. Dyneema was developed in the late 1970s for chemical companies in search of a strong synthetic fibre suitable for aerospace and military applications. It went on to be used for products that call for extreme strength, a lightweight construction and a high degree of abrasion resistance. Examples are helmets, bulletproof vests, rope, nets, hockey sticks, tennis rackets, gloves, fishing line, kite string and protective panelling for cars. Dyneema is available as yarn, fabric and sheeting (Dyneema UD). Also of interest is Dyneema Fraglight, a strong, felt-like material used to make impact-resistant tents.

52

INFLATABLE WALL

Composition
Polyester or PVC

Properties
Ultra-light, easy to assemble, reusable, double-walled

Applications
Exhibitions, stands, public events

Contact
Braun Wagner
Krefelderstrasse 147
D-52070 Aachen
Germany
T +49 (0)2419 973 960
F +49 (0)2419 973 961
info@braunwagner.de
www.braunwagner.de

Photo
Loewe's trade-fair stand at CEBIT 2002 relies on airwall technology developed by Braun Wagner.

Manfred Wagner and Ralf Braun's airwall, which features double-walled membranes of PVC or polyester spinnaker fabric, provides an interesting solution for temporary applications like exhibitions, stands and public events. The lightweight, easy-to-transport airwall construction can be erected in minutes.
Braun Wagner used inflatable PVC airwalls (M1 fire-resistant) to build a 5-metre-high circular theatre for the Canon Millennium Event at the Louvre (Paris, 2000). Built in only three days, the evnet – a multimedia world that explored Canon's innovative potential on 4500 square metres – was based on the 'plug and play' philosophy. Composed of individual cells, the structure boasted a built-in, adjust- able, time-regulated lighting system. Loewe used inflatable volumes of spinnaker fabric (B1 fire-resistant) for its IFA stand (Berlin, 2001), as well as for a modular system that has appeared at various European trade fairs.

LOEWE.
LOEWE.
LOEWE.
LOEWE.
Just one zap to internet.

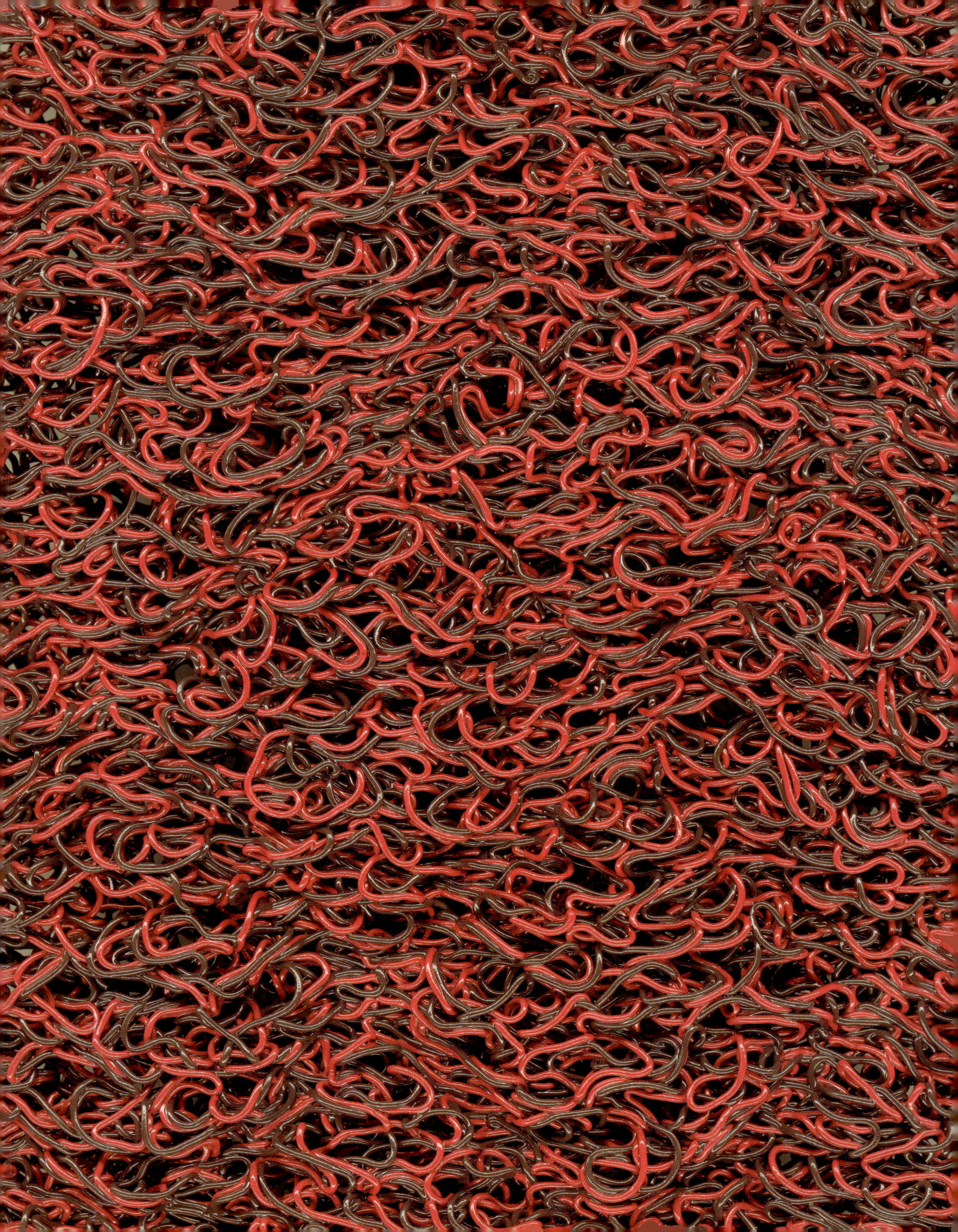

53

AESTHETIC ENTRANCE FLOORING

Composition
Vinyl fibres

Properties
Nonslip, durable, UV-resistant, impervious to most chemical substances, allows moisture to pass through

Applications
Entrances to public buildings, including shops and offices

Technical specifications
www.bonarfloors.com/coral

Contact
Bonar Floors
High Holborn Road
Ripley
Derbyshire DE5 3NT
UK
T +44 (0)1773 744 121
F +44 (0)1773 744 142
bonarfloors.uk@lowandbonar.com
www.bonarfloors.com

Photo
Thanks to colourful interwoven loops of vinyl, the Coral Grip clean-off system presents an attractive image.

Coral Grip is a clean-off system with a nonwoven, textured structure of fused vinyl fibres. The open structure of this highly flexible material lets moisture pass through. Brightly coloured vinyl-fibre loops give Coral Grip an aesthetic character.
The product, which functions as a dirt remover, can be installed on top of existing flooring. Because it stops walked-in soil and moisture, Coral Grip is ideal for busy public entrances. The system greatly reduces cleaning costs and extends the life span of other floor coverings.
Coral Grip comes in rolls (122 cm x 6 m) and individual mats (60 x 90 cm) with a patented, textured, checked design.

54

FIBRE-REINFORCED COMPOSITE SYSTEM

Composition
Fabric made of E-glass, Kevlar, carbon fibre or a hybrid of these materials; Tyfo S epoxy

Properties
Lightweight, bendable, flexible, offers protection (from collisions, explosions, earthquakes, corrosion, water and insect damage), equal in strength to concrete and steel up to 20 cm thick, easy to use, no loss of space, has little effect on appearance, cost-saving and convenient (in comparison with standard alternatives)

Applications
Bridges, roads, buildings (reinforcement of structural members like beams, plain and reinforced concrete volumes, walls, slabs, wooden piles, pipes)

Technical specifications
www.fyfeco.com/tyfosys.html

Contact
Fyfe Co. LLC
Nancy Ridge Technology Center
6310 Nancy Ridge Drive, Suite 103
San Diego CA 92121
USA
T +1 858 642 0694
F +1 858 642 0947
info@fyfeco.com
www.fyfeco.com

Photo
High-strength composite fibres like Tyfo Fibrwrap have emerged as an efficient method for reinforcing, repairing and protecting concrete and masonry structures.

Tyfo Fibrwrap features a strong fabric with a varied composition (contains E-glass, Kevlar, carbon fibre or a hybrid of these materials), which is impregnated with epoxy resin. The thickness of one layer varies from 0.035 to 0.129 cm. The material is used to increase the strength and ductility of bridges, buildings and other structures. The composition of the fabric is geared to a specific project and to the foundation to which the material is to be applied.
Installing the product is a four-step process. First the foundation must be repaired, if needed, cleaned and painted with an epoxy primer. Next a special saturator impregnates the cheesecloth-like material, on site, with epoxy; when completely saturated, the wrap is applied. Sometimes several layers of material are applied, including wraps that offer protection from UV light, fire and/or toxic waste. The final step involves a finishing coat that can be mixed to match existing colours.
The Fibrwrap technique is ideal for the reinforcement and repair of hard-to-access spots, such as bridge piers and building foundations. Small crews (three to five men) using hand tools can prepare and install Tyfo composite systems. Noise is minimal and only small sections of a facility are affected at one time.
Adopted from the military and aeronautical industries (the Stealth bomber has a skin of this material), Tyfo Fibrwrap has been used to reinforce, repair and protect a wide variety of architectural, civil and other infrastructures. The system allows columns to bend as much as 20 cm without cracking; it withstands earthquakes with a magnitude up to 6.7. Because the technique is virtually undetectable to the naked eye, a structure can be reinforced with no significant alteration in architecture or appearance. Retrofitted elements shaped like rectangles, octagons, squares and ovals retain their original form.

55

CLIMATE-CONTROL SCREENS

Composition
Aluminium, polyester

Properties
Flexible, UV-resistant, antistatic, lets light and moisture pass through, reflects heat, saves energy, is unaffected by chemicals, requires only infrequent cleaning

Applications
Horticulture

Contact
Ludvig Svensson
Bangatan 8
SE-511 82 Kinna
Sweden
T +46 (0)320 209 200
F +46 (0)320 211 010
info@ludvigsvensson.com
www.ludvigsvensson.com

Photo
XLS screens provide climate control and energy management for greenhouses.

Svensson's energy-saving XLS screens control light, temperature and humidity in all types of greenhouses. After installation, the screens can be opened and closed. The product features 4-mm-wide aluminium and polyester strips held together by a webbing of strong, transparent polyester thread. These are effective materials for the reflection and transmission of light and heat. Thanks to the webbed structure, XLS screens let enough moisture pass through to prevent an undesirable accumulation of humidity and condensation on the underside of the screen. The flexible screen can be rolled up to allow a maximum amount of light to enter the greenhouse.
XLS comes is a variety of standard widths. Special widths can be supplied upon request. The fabric is sold by length and as a ready-made roller blind.

SOU
NDC
ONT
ROL

INTRO

Decades ago the walls of sound studios were clad with egg cartons to dampen unwanted reverberations. Much of the commercial sound insulation used today is just as unsightly as that makeshift solution. In the past, manufacturers took it for granted that soundproofing materials would be an invisible aspect of any project requiring them.

That viewpoint is changing. A new generation of soundproofing materials makes a deliberate attempt to be a visual feature of design: technology becomes decoration. Manufactured in Sweden by Snowcrash, Soundwave is a series of wall tiles of moulded polyester fibre. Soundwave tiles, which have striking threedimensional surfaces, are backed with self-adhesive pads for easy mounting; the tiles can be removed and reapplied elsewhere. Simple vacuuming keeps them clean.

Other innovative products are completely invisible when in use. German firm Troplast, for example, developed a flexible acoustic film for laminated safety glass that leaves the glazed surface to which it is applied perfectly transparent. The film affects neither clarity nor light stability.

And as seen so often in the world of materials, here too design and architecture can benefit from sound-control technology gleaned from other sectors. Think of the automotive industry, which invests a great deal of time and money in sound- and energy-absorbing materials to reduce noise pollution inside cars and other vehicles. Other manufacturers do their utmost to make household appliances like washing machines, dryers and dishwashers as quiet as possible, particularly because today's flexitime system has prompted a round-the-clock use of such domestic aids. Acoustic techniques developed by the makers of cars and household appliances are a potential source of inspiration for interior architects.

56

METAL SANDWICH SHEET

Composition
Viscose elastic polymer, metal

Properties
Fully recyclable, insulating, fully weldable, thin, flexible, reduces noise and vibration

Applications
Automotive (engines, body structures, brakes, brackets), public transport (trucks, buses, aircraft, boats, ships), power equipment (lawn mowers, generators), household appliances (dishwashers, water coolers, washers, dryers), electronic components (printers, copy machines, disk drives, coin counters)

Technical specifications
Downloads via
www.laminatesandcomposites.com

Contact
MSC Laminates and Composites
2300 East Pratt Blvd.
Elk Grove Village IL 60007-5995
USA
T +1 847 439 1822
F +1 847 806 2219
www.laminatesandcomposites.com

Photo
Quiet Steel dampens vibration over a wide range of temperatures by transferring vibrational energy – either by mechanical extension and contraction or by shearing – into thermal energy.

This family of sound- and noise-damping, constrained-layer materials features a core of viscose elastic thermoplastic sandwiched between two or three metal skins. Known as Quiet Steel, the product dampens vibration over a wide range of temperatures by transferring vibrational energy – either by mechanical extension and contraction or by shearing – into thermal energy. Thanks to the high loss factor, impact noise can be reduced by 10 to 20 dB and noise from boundary-exited vibration by 3 to 8 dB. The eco-friendly product can be electroplated and galvanised; it tolerates temperatures up to 418°C and is completely recyclable.
Supplied as rolled sheet, Quiet Steel has a 0.025-mm-thick polymer core that allows the material to be used for standard sheet-metal processing techniques like slitting, roll forming, drawing and punching. The structural integrity of the end product is determined by the choice of metal and thickness, while the polymer core can be tailored to meet specific noise-reduction needs.
The relatively lightweight, cost-saving composite is suitable for automotive engine parts and dashboards. The electronics industry is using Quiet Steel to make vibration-reducing disk covers, direct access storage device (DASD) cages and disk drive brackets. Another application is the manufacture of household appliances such as dishwashers and washing machines.

SP(SB)

57

HONEYCOMB FOAM

Composition
Polyolefin

Properties
Sound-absorbent, recyclable (releases no poisonous gases when burnt), highly elastic, can be shaped to any design during expansion, suitable for secondary thermoforming

Applications
Underlay for laminate flooring

Technical specifications
www.reviro.com

Contact
Sekisui Chemical
Business, 3-4-7 Toranomon,
Minato-ku
Tokyo 105-8450
Japan
T +81 (0)3 3434 9075
F +81 (0)3 3434 9078
www.sekisui.co.jp

Photo
Honeycomb foam is used as a sound-absorbent underlay for wooden flooring.

Honeycomb foam is made by expanding close-packed pellets of polyolefin with the use of a foaming agent that has a high expansion coefficient. The resulting material has an extremely elastic honeycomb structure from top to bottom (a thickness of 5 to 6 mm) and is rigid along the sides. It can be roll formed or made into curved surfaces without moulding.
The Japanese manufacturer calls its products Lee bi-Ro and Reviro.
When used as an underlay for wooden flooring, honeycomb foam reduces noise, dampens vibrations and provides extra insulation. Foam panels come in white, black and grey and in sizes up to 1 x 2 m. Customised dimensions are available on orders over 100 kg.

58

LIGHT-WEIGHT ENERGY ABSORBER

Composition
Metals, thermoplastics or thermosetting plastics

Properties
Lightweight, economical, energy-absorbing, recyclable, easily formed, displays excellent angular behaviour, has a better bending and torsion stress between two skins than aluminium honeycomb, lends itself to series production

Applications
Automotive and pedestrian protection: A, B and C pillars; roof lining, grab handles, foot protection, side impact, bonnets, bumpers, front wings

Technical specifications
Download PDF via www.cellbond.com

Contact
Cellbond Composites
5 Stukeley Business Centre
Blackstone Road
Huntingdon
Cambridgeshire PE29 6EF
UK
T +44 (0)1480 435 302
F +44 (0)1480 432 019
sales@cellbond.com
www.cellbond.co.uk

Photo
Thanks to their unique design, these lightweight panels absorb a great deal of the energy produced when two vehicles collide.

PressLoad is the brand name that Cellbond Composites uses for its lightweight, energy-absorbent panels and tiles. Thermoformed and cold pressed from aluminium alloys, polycarbonate, acrylonitrile butadiene styrene, polypropylene and other materials, these products rely on a specially designed geometry for their excellent energy-absorbing characteristics. Similar to that of an egg carton, the structure of the material consists of protrusions and hollows that form an impact-absorbent surface particularly beneficial in the event of a collision. Custom-manufactured sheets of this material can be made as large as 1.5 x 3 m.
The easily formed PressLoad structure is suitable for application in the automotive industry, where panels made of this energy-absorbing material can replace the rigid foam traditionally used for fenders, seats, dashboards and the like. The performance of conventional absorbers does not always meet today's strict legal requirements and growing public expectations. The cost of the panels is comparable to that of foam, and PressLoad takes up less packaging space.

59

SOUND-CONTROL FILM

Composition
Polyvinyl butyral

Properties
Sound-suppressing (37dB), reinforces impact resistance

Applications
Primarily industrial constructions

Technical specifications
www.trosifol.com/eng/products/trosifol_sc.html

Contact
HT Troplast
Produktbereich Trosifol
Mülheimerstrasse 26
D-53840 Troisdorf
Germany
T +49 (0)2241 853 214
F +49 (0)2241 853 488
www.trosifol.com

Photo
Trosifol Sound Control film, used here at Terminal 2 of the Cologne-Bonn Airport, increases the safety of glazed façades and reduces noise pollution. Photography by Cologne-Bonn Airport.

Trosifol Sound Control is a flexible polyvinyl-butyral film for laminated safety glass. The material considerably reduces sound transmission (37dB) and is as easy to apply as standard interlayers used in the manufacture of laminated safety glass.
Multiple glazing is widely recognised for the excellent thermal insulation it provides. However, growing noise levels, particularly in cities, are demanding that glazing – used extensively for building façades and other architectural elements – provide acoustic insulation as well. Less noise pollution means less emotional and psychological stress.
Applied to laminated safety glass, sound-control film adds the advantage of improved sound reduction to the final product. The film has no adverse effect on clarity, transparency and/or light stability. The 0.76-mm-thick material is available in 200-m-long rolls with standard widths of 120 to 321 cm. An interlayer of PE prevents the PVB sheets from sticking together at room temperature.

60

POROUS CONSTRUCTION MATERIAL

Composition
Granules made of recycled materials (sintered coal ashes, clay, glass shards, eco grid, etc.), powder paint

Properties
Highly sound-absorbent, lightweight (compared with concrete), strong, weather-resistant (tolerates frost), chemical-resistant, eco-friendly, recyclable, inexpensive, easy to clean, available in varying degrees of porosity, provides good insulation

Applications
(dependent on the type of granules used)
Panelling (walls, floors and ceilings of offices, factories, swimming pools, saunas and gymnasiums), sandwich components, acoustic barriers (motorways, tunnels), building façades

Contact
Ten Berge Coating Systems
Rijnhavenkade 2
NL-2404 HB Alphen aan den Rijn
The Netherlands
T +31 (0)172 478 888
F +31 (0)172 478 181
info@tenberge.nl
www.tenberge.nl

Photo
Porous Construction Material is a sound-absorbent product in which granules of recycled material are fused together with powder paint.

Porocom, which stands for porous construction material, is an environmentally friendly product that reduces noise pollution. It consists of granules made of recycled materials. The granules are heated to a temperature of about 200°C and then brought into contact with thermosetting powder paint, a residue of the manufacture of coatings. The paint quickly covers the granules, but does not completely harden at this point. The coated granules, a semimanufactured product, are marketed as Porocom. The end product is made by sintering the granules in a mould, causing them to stick together and achieve maximum hardness. As a building composite, Porocom is suitable for use in indoor and outdoor nonbearing constructions. The degree of porosity is established by varying the temperature at which granules combine with the residual powder. The resulting product can range from a high-density structure to one with a cell structure of 30 per cent. The sintering process is a one-step operation that allows Porocom to bind with other materials, such as sheet metal, to form a composite suitable as panelling for exterior walls.
Ten Berge has used Porocom in developing a flat sheet metal, as well as a self-supporting, sound-absorbing element (Tremolo) with ridges separated by grooves that can be filled with mineral wool.

61

SHOCK-ABSORBING FOAM

Composition
Polyester

Properties
Sound-absorbent, high density, open-pored (easily soiled), flexible, strong, returns to original shape after compaction

Applications
Health care (mattresses, cushions, earplugs), architectural construction

Contact
Swisstex
PO Box 9258
Greenville SC 29604-9258
USA
T +1 864 845 7541
F +1 864 845 5699
swissinfo@sprintmail.com
www.swisstex.com

Beige Design
The Tannery
738 Gilman Street
Berkeley CA 94710
USA
T +1 510 525 9602
F +1 510 525 9672
info@beigedesign.com
www.beigedesign.com

Photo
Thom Faulders of Beige Design used shock-absorbing foam (SAF) for a three-dimensional installation that invites visitors to lounge and listen to music. He achieved the desired effect, while also lowering the cost of his project, by laminating 25-mm-thick SAF onto 100-mm-thick flexible, low-grade polyurethane foam. Photography by Kevin Dwarka.

Shock-absorbing foams (SAFs) made of polyester are distinguishable from conventional foams because of their pronounced viscous-elastic behaviour. The reaction of the material varies with the rate of application of force: this foam reacts to gradual force with a viscous behaviour, whereas shock-like force produces elastic behaviour. The viscous-elastic behaviour is strongly dependent on temperature (the foam becomes more pliable with warmth, as from the body) and humidity.
Because SAFs help prevent bedsores, they are often used in the manufacture of orthopaedic and medical mattresses and cushions. The material ensures uniform pressure distribution even with heavy loading and offers a support similar to gel or liquid cushions. The relatively open-pored foam structure can 'breathe': it provides good air circulation and reduces excessive perspiration. For protection and for reasons of hygiene, mattress and cushion covers are recommended. SAF underlays and overlays can be washed, machine-dried and autoclaved.
Thom Faulders of Beige Design fashioned an intriguing installation with SAF for the Rooms for Listening exhibition (California College of Arts and Crafts), which featured a spectrum of experimental electronic music and sound. The installation, called Mute Room, is composed of 1800 square feet of pink memory foam (SAF 60120), enough to fill the entire gallery like a fleshy hill, a gently rolling landscape coaxing visitors to walk around, sit down and curl on its surface. Crossing the foam surface is like walking on wet sand, footprints gradually fading away. The 'smart foam' erases itself while retaining the original imprint in its memory. It contours to a shape, typically a body part, giving both a satisfying feel and a high degree of support. The material creates an ideal lounging environment for experimental electronic music: the room becomes a cushion in which the music is paramount.

62

SOUND-ABSORBING PANELS

Composition
Moulded polyester fibre or PET

Properties
Sound-absorbent, versatile, tactile, easy to clean

Applications
Interior walls, suspended screens, freestanding space dividers, backdrop for plasma screens

Technical specifications
Downloads via www.snowcrash.se/downloads

Contact
Snowcrash
Textilvägen 1
SE-120 30 Stockholm
Sweden
T +46 (0)8 442 9810
F +46 (0)8 442 9811
info@snowcrash.se
www.snowcrash.se

Photo
Soundwave is a sound-absorbent panel attractive enough to be used as a surfacing material.

Soundwave is an acoustic material made primarily of moulded polyester fibre. The product has an interesting three-dimensional form. Generally speaking, sound-absorbent materials used in interior design are not attractive enough to remain in view. Soundwave, however, combines functionality and aesthetics to make acoustic control a visible dimension of environmental design.
The Soundwave series features three sculptural panels – Swoop, Swell and Scrunch – each designed for a specific acoustic purpose. A number of like panels mounted in a row creates a rhythmic pattern with a tactile appeal. Swoop is a heavyweight sound absorber designed to reduce disturbing background noise (sound bouncing around) and to improve voice intelligibility. This panel is very efficient in the low-frequency range (150-500 Hz). Its surface, which looks like stone, is dotted with small cavities. Swell and Scrunch are lightweight sound absorbers designed for the high-frequency range (500 Hz and above). They help reduce environmental sound like voices and telephones. Swell has a convex surface, while Scrunch is characterised by a rock-like appearance. Swell and Scrunch can also be used as screens to improve privacy in open-plan interiors.
A fourth model, Swell Diffuser, has a glossy finish and a completely different function. Made completely of PET, this panel amplifies sound rather than absorbing it.
Self-adhesive Velcro pads are attached to the back of each panel, making the panels easy to mount and easy to move from one spot to another. They can be cleaned with a vacuum cleaner or gently brushed by hand. Available colours are anthracite, grey, off-white and sand. Each panel weighs from 1 to 1.5 kg and is 8 cm thick and 58.5 cm square.

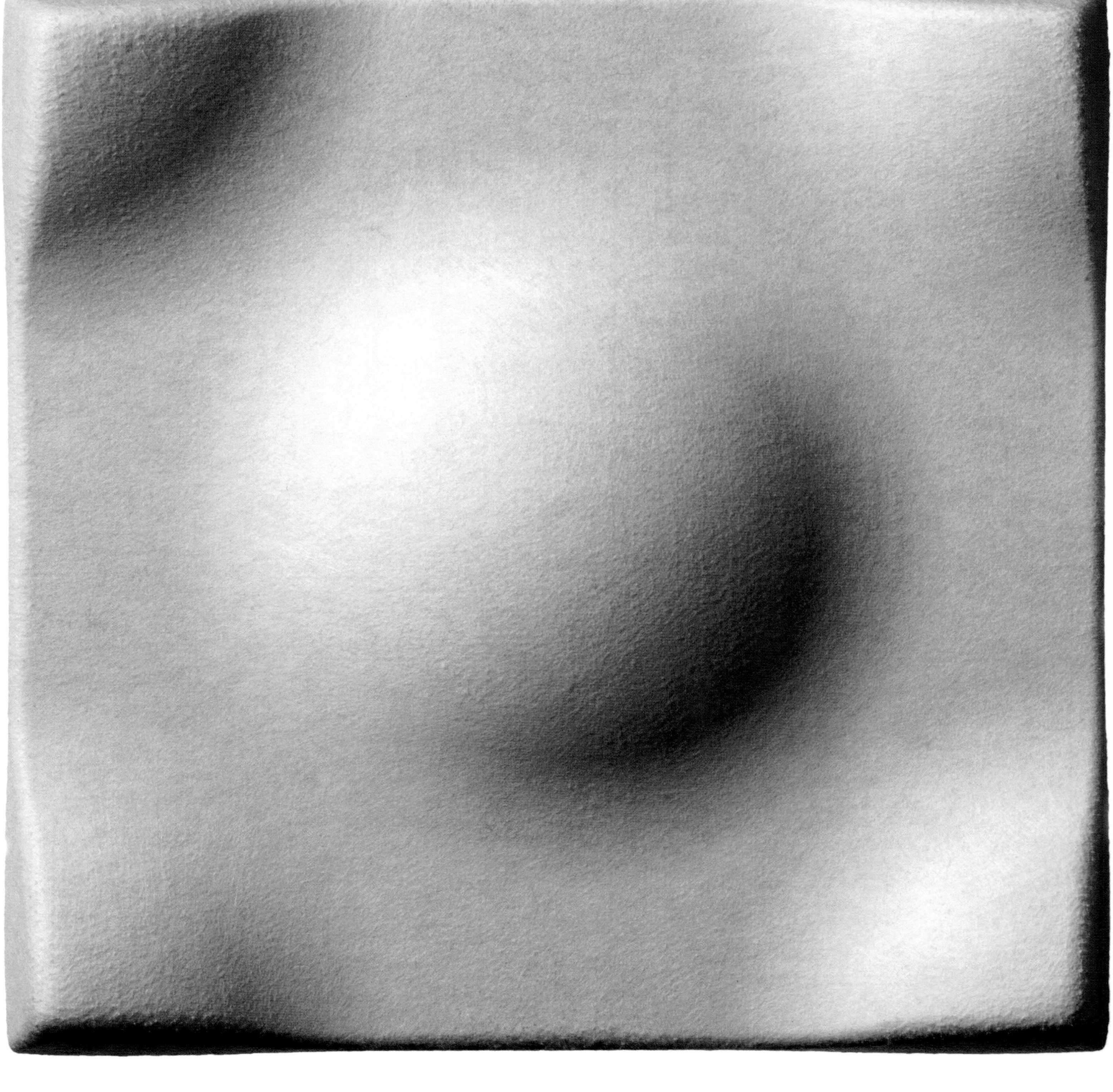

STR ONG BUIL DING

INTRO

A major challenge facing architecture and design is the problem of how to make constructions lighter without making them weaker. Modern materials with a high strength-to-weight ratio are the solution. Most of these materials were developed in America for the aerospace industry and the United States Navy, where they are used to make light, strong, impact-resistant bodies and hulls for planes and ships.

Recently, honeycomb structures have also made their way into architecture. A number of companies have developed composite materials that feature a honeycomb structure of aluminium or cardboard, for example, sandwiched by transparent, translucent or opaque layers of substances such as glass, polymer, carbon fibre and fibreglass. Applications include doors, table pods, room dividers and flooring. Honeycomb structures combined with light can be used to create beautiful optical effects.

Equally lightweight, strong and rigid is a spongy material known as stabilised aluminium foam. It is used in the automotive industry, among others, as reinforcement for the chassis and as a shock absorber in bonnets, doors and boots. Two other obvious applications of this material are architectural components and furniture design.

Architects are experimenting with solid materials that are light in a figurative sense. Still in an early phase of development, translucent-transparent concrete resembles conventional concrete in all but appearance.

Were such a product to appear on the market, the consequences for architecture would be enormous: designers would have the opportunity to replace windows with bearing walls that allow light to enter the building.

Less high-tech, but already realised in the Netherlands, is a house made of sheets of glass glued together.

In addition to solid materials, today's market offers the designer super-strong, flexible fibres. A good example is Dyneema, a stronger-than-steel material used in the manufacture of canvas, bulletproof cockpit doors, helmets and impact-resistant tents. Special composite fabrics, such as Tyfo Fibrwrap, are used to wrap disintegrating and unstable sections of concrete structures like bridges and building foundations. This remedy reinforces the wrapped section and protects it from outside influences, including earthquakes. The fabric is impregnated with a special epoxy resin that not only makes it strong, but also causes the material to adhere to concrete.

The development of super fibres is still in the early stages. Scientists are currently studying the exact composition of what may be the strongest material on earth: the cobweb. As soon as industry is able to reproduce and mass-produce the strong filament spun by certain spiders, innovations in the fields of architecture and design will not be far behind.

63

TRANS-LUCENT HONEYCOMB PANEL

Composition
Aluminium or polymer core, fibreglass-reinforced acrylic facings

Properties
Translucent, high strength-to-weight ratio, low-maintenance, weather- and scratch-resistant, easy to handle, cut, drill and machine

Applications
Tabletops, partition walls, sliding doors, ceiling components

Contact
Panelite
600 Broadway, Suite 4c
New York NY 10012
USA
T +1 212 343 0995
F +1 212 343 8187
info@e-panelite.com
www.e-panelite.com

Photo
Translucent honeycomb panels combine the architectural potential of translucence with the structural performance of an aerospace technology that uses honeycomb structures for their low weight and high degree of stiffness.

Translucent honeycomb panels have a strong, lightweight aluminium or polymer honeycomb core and fibreglass-reinforced acrylic facings in clear, white or blue. The panels combine the architectural potential of translucence with the structural performance of an aerospace technology that uses honeycomb core structures for their very low weight and high degree of stiffness. The honeycomb structure comes in four designs: hexagonal, overexpanded, tube and weave. The top layer is low-maintenance, as well as weather- and scratch-resistant.
The aesthetic effect of Panelite relies heavily on the degree to which natural or artificial light can penetrate or be reflected by the translucent material, whose coloration reacts to luminous intensity and angle of incidence. Panels can be doubled to achieve greater opacity.
Thanks to their honeycomb structure, the panels require minimal framing supports. But the untreated and often vulnerable edge of a honeycomb composite must be protected to ensure optimum performance. Rails make the system even more adaptable. Working with the material calls for conventional woodworking methods. Panels are available in two sizes: 1.22 x 2.44 m and 1.22 x 3.05 m. The size of the honeycomb cell is 9.6 mm. The aluminium core is 1.91 cm thick.

64

LAMINATED GLASS SHEETS

Composition
Glass sheets (10mm), dual-component silicone glue

Properties
Strong, translucent, expensive, produces a chromatic effect, transparent only when viewed at right angles, collects heat and thus prevents an overheated interior

Applications
Interior and exterior walls, ceilings and floors

Contact
Kruunenberg Van der Erve Architects
Conradstraat 8
NL-1018 NG Amsterdam
The Netherlands
T +31 (0)20 320 8486
kvdearch@wxs.nl

Saint-Gobain Glass Nederland
PO Box 507
NL-3900 AM Veenendaal
The Netherlands
T +31 (0)318 531 311
F +31 (0)736 413 925
www.saint-gobain.com

Photo
Laminata, a prefab house designed by Kruunenberg Van der Erve Architects and located in the Dutch town of Leerdam, is built almost completely of glass. Photography by Arjen Schmitz.

Sheets of glass glued together make a good building material. Constructed almost entirely of laminated glass, the experimental prefab building in the Dutch town of Leerdam designed by Kruunenberg Van der Erve Architects is a remarkable study into the spatial and structural qualities of glass. Laminata (the name of the building) reads as a massively solid block of glazing out of which individual rooms have been carved. Thousands of identical glass sheets are arranged back to back to form an oblong, solid mass of glass, which is then cut lengthways. No less than 80m2 of glass went into the building, enough glazing for around 80 conventional houses. The laminated glass sheets are used for external and internal walls, which vary from 10 to an incredible 170 cm in thickness. Despite their massiveness, the walls still transmit light.
Preliminary research for the Laminata project, carried out in collaboration with TNO Delft and Saint-Gobain, took four years. The dual-component silicone glue had to be permanently flexible, UV-resistant and damp-proof; it needed the same refractive index as glass. The material was tested for weathering, temperature variations, algal growth and fresh-water immersion.
To create an environment with a controlled temperature and a stable level of humidity while gluing the sheets of glass together, the building site was covered during most of the construction. Ultimately, the sheets were lined up 'along the plumb line', one by one, and moved into position. Traction tests were done on site to determine the strength of the bond between glass sheets and aluminium components glued together. (Metal components were needed to connect walls and roof.) An on-site study also revealed how much light and heat passes through glass walls of various thicknesses. Glass in such massive quantities eliminates the need for air conditioning, which a house with traditional glass walls would require.

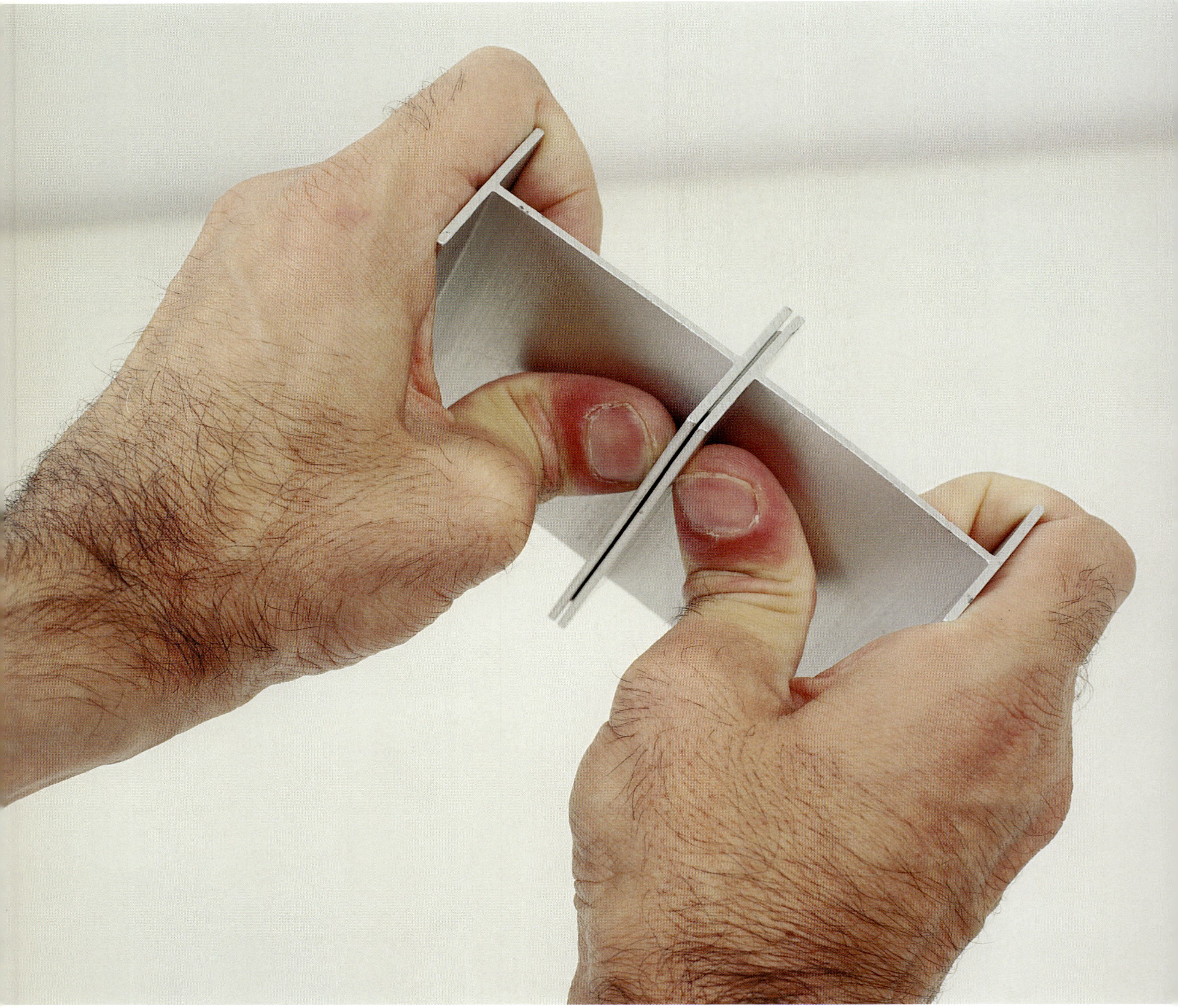

65

VERY HIGH BOND TAPE

Composition
Tape, white acrylic adhesive

Properties
Strong, viscoelastic, temperature-resistant, damps vibration and noise, reduces costs, is suitable for irregular surfaces, leaves basic structure undamaged, produces a durable bond, assembly is fast and easy, creates beautiful finished surfaces, uniform thickness (from 0.6 to 3 mm)

Applications
Transport, aviation, space travel, electronics, outdoor advertising, metal and plastics industries, construction, architecture, interiors

Technical specifications
Downloads via www.3m.com

Contact
3M Nederland
Bonding Systems & Adhesives for Electronic & Converter Markets
PO Box 193
NL-2300 AD Leiden
The Netherlands
T +31 (0)71 545 0552
F +31 (0)71 545 0597

Photo
Very high bond tape (VHB) has a high degree of adhesive strength on both sides.

Very high bond (VHB) tape is a double-sided product that creates a strong connection. The material consists of a homogeneous layer of closed-cell foam composed completely of an extremely adhesive acrylic that resists stress, fatigue, vibration, heat, cold, temperature cycling, moisture, solvents and UV light. When applied to irregular surfaces, normal tape adheres only to the upper layer. The continuous bond created by VHB's acrylic adhesive penetrates every pore of an uneven surface, thus distributing stress along the entire surface and creating a much stronger bond than that provided by alternative products.
Its viscoelastic property allows VHB to absorb impact, relax stress and damp vibration over a wide range of temperatures. The user-friendly material eliminates the need for welding, drilling, riveting and screw fastening, while saving time and money.
Thanks to its completely closed-cell structure, the tape creates a protective barrier that seals liquids and gases in or out.
VHB is used in trains, trucks and buses for joining interior and exterior panels invisibly and for damping vibration. In the aircraft industry, the tape is used to bond protective, stainless-steel strips to the aluminium landing flaps of aeroplanes, a connection that remains unaffected by extreme ground and air temperatures. Owing to its adhesive strength, resistance to weather, easy assembly and invisibility, VHB is used to fasten panels and windows to exterior walls.

66

TRANS-LUCENT OR TRANS-PARENT CONCRETE

Composition
Glass, polymerised synthetics

Properties
Translucent, transparent, strong, potentially cost-saving

Applications
Structural building elements (floors, walls, columns and beams), interior fixtures, 3-D castings

Contact
Bill Price
12110 Queensbury Lane
Houston TX 77024
USA
T +1 713 743 2400
billpprice@hotmail.com

Photo
A new type of concrete attempts to combine translucence or transparency with the normal properties of concrete: solidity and flexibility. Photography by Kennon Evett.

Still an experimental material, translucent or transparent concrete is concrete in all but appearance.
It attempts to combine the quality of 'light passing through' with the normal properties of concrete: solidity and flexibility. The objective is to make buildings that glow from within without any visible obstacles – structures that do not need supporting beams or joints. The material is meant to form an alternative for reinforced structures with traditional glazing. The manufacturing method would remain the same. Although the cost may be five times higher than traditional concrete, one could save money on those materials made obsolete by the new technology. Seen as such, the material is a financially attractive solution. A handful of experimental building projects using derivatives or offspring from research done on this material are currently in the works.
Translucent or transparent concrete may be the key to a totally new way of thinking about architecture.

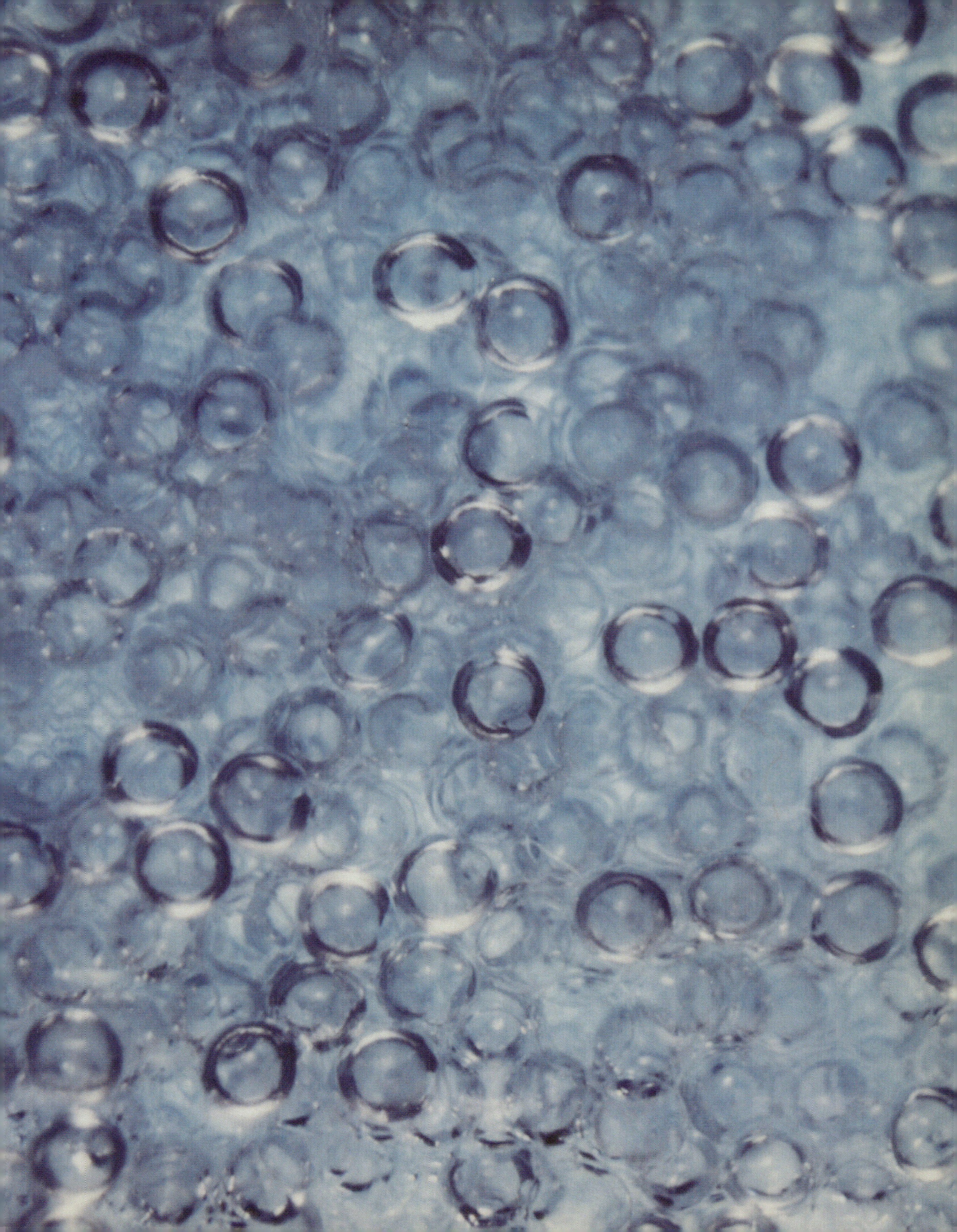

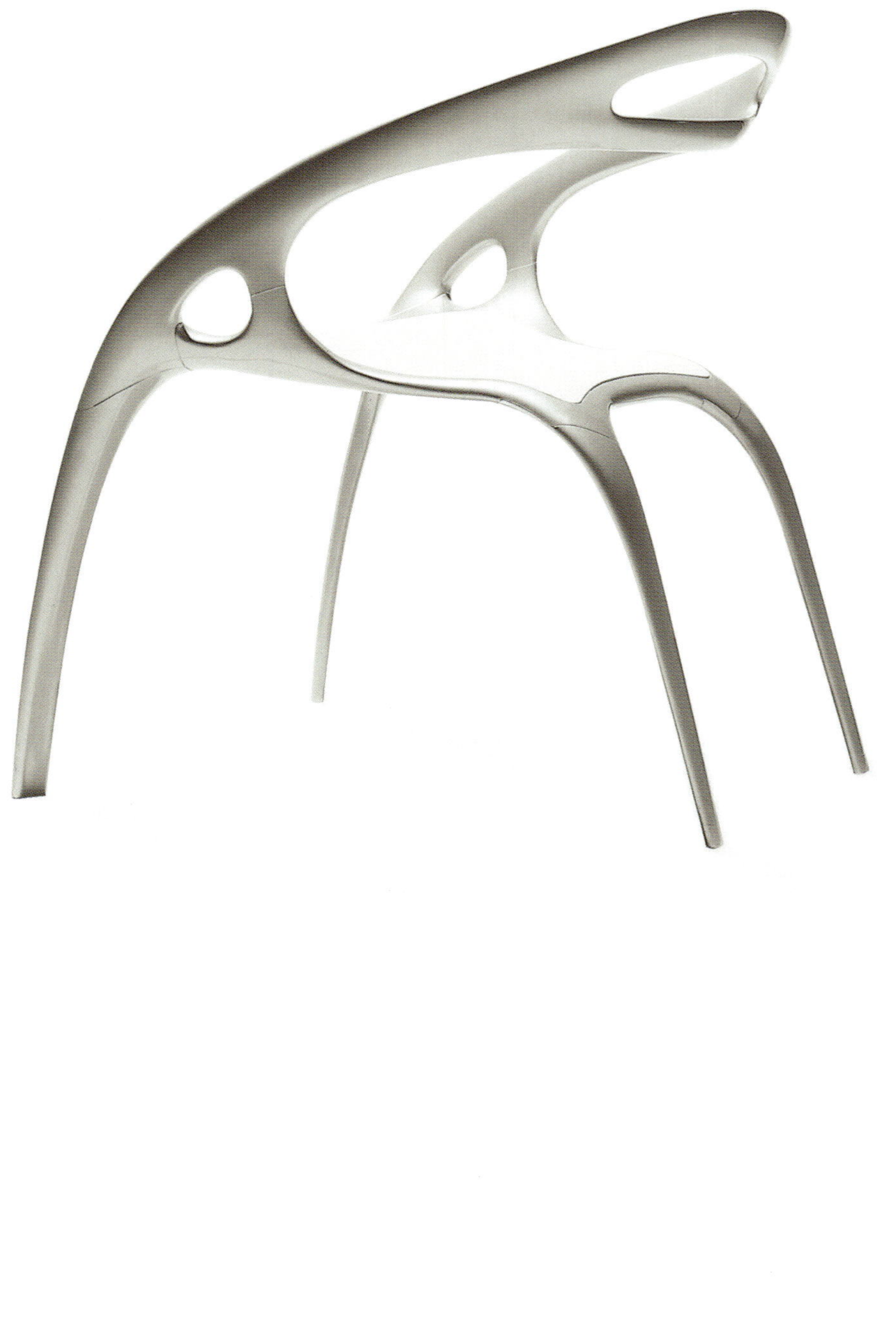

67

INJECTION-MOULDED MAGNESIUM

Composition
Powder-coated magnesium

Properties
High strength-to-weight ratio, provides good insulation, is easy to machine

Applications
Automotive industry, furniture

Contact
Bernhardt Design
1839 Morganton Blvd.
Lenoir NC 28645
USA
T +1 828 758 9811
F +1 828 759 6259
www.bernhardtdesign.com

Ross Lovegrove
21 Powis Mews
London W11 1JN
UK
T +44 (0)20 7229 7104
F +44 (0)20 7229 7032
studiox@compuserve.com

Photo
Designed by Ross Lovegrove, the Go chair is made of injection-moulded magnesium, which makes it lightweight but strong.

Lighter than aluminium, magnesium possesses the highest strength-to-weight ratio of any of the commonly used metals. Injection-moulded magnesium turns up regularly inside planes, cars and power tools and, thanks to its insulating qualities and easy machinability, is finding a host of new applications, such as computer-shielding plates and extruded profiles.

Furniture designers are also showing an interest in the material. A good example is Ross Lovegrove, who created the Go collection of tables and chairs for Bernhardt Design. The Go chair is a curvaceously streamlined, sculptural construction that mimics the physiology of the human form. The carved-out voids save both material and weight, but not at the expense of strength. The first version of the chair, made of aluminium, weighed over 12.71 kg: too heavy for its solid metal construction. After looking for new manufacturing methods and materials, Bernhardt Design rejected titanium in favour of an even lighter option: magnesium. The magnesium frame of the chair relies on an injection-moulding technique borrowed from the automotive industry, which uses it to make light, strong and durable cars. Go chair's six cast-magnesium 'bones' are fused together with machine screws and industrial adhesives.

The definitive version of Go chair weighs about 6.81 kg. Because magnesium oxidises and ultimately turns black, the naturally rough surface of the metal is powder-coated (silver or white) to create a gleaming finish. The standard frame accommodates seats upholstered in fabric, as well as seats made of polycarbonate or wood.

68

COMPOSITE GLASS FLOORING

Composition
Structural glass, aluminium

Properties
Strong, transparent, nonslip (thanks to sandblasted surface or strips)

Applications
flooring, stairs, banisters, stages, partitions, doors, screening

Technical specification
www.cellbond.com

Contact
Cellbond Architectural
5 Stukeley Business Centre
Blackstone Road
Huntingdon
Cambridgeshire PE29 6EF
UK
T +44 (0)1480 435 302
F +44 (0)1480 432 019
sales@cellbond.com
www.cellbond.co.uk

Photo
B-Clear Glass Flooring, a composite structural glass panel with an aluminium honeycomb structure, is lighter, stiffer and stronger than comparable glass products.

B-Clear Glass Flooring is a composite structural glass panel with an aluminium honeycomb structure. The largest panel is 300 x 150 cm; thickness ranges from 25 to 50 mm. The toughened glass itself is 4mm thick.
The honeycomb structure has a cell size of 20 mm and a cell height of 17 to 19 mm. The self-weight of a 25-to-27-mm panel is 20 kg/m2. Finishes are clear, sandblasted and/or coloured. Vibration from foot traffic has been limited by testing the fundamental frequency of the panel under inertial loads greater than or equal to 5 Hz.
While specially developed for use in flooring, the product is suitable for a range of other applications. Lighter, stiffer and stronger than comparable glass products, the panels combine the safety features and good looks valued by those in the retail, leisure and domestic sectors. A polycarbonate version of the product (B-Clear Poly) is suitable for vertical applications only. Openings for fibre-optic illumination can create special effects and add a decorative touch to the end result. Various edge details are possible: grey filler, flush natural anodised aluminium, clear and natural anodised aluminium U-channel.

69

PANELS WITH A CELLULAR STRUCTURE

Composition
Various combinations of aluminium, polycarbonate, Kevlar, carbon fibre, fibreglass, polyester

Properties
Transparent, durable, UV-resistant (if desired), fire-resistant, impact-resistant, lightweight, provides sound control

Applications
Sliding doors, table pods, room dividers, back panelling, fixturing, flooring (phenolic)

Contact
Airframe Advanced Materials
1003 Boston Post Road
Darien CT 06802
USA
T +1 203 656 7223
F +1 203 655 6423
www.airframeusa.com

Photo
Panels with a cellular structure are lightweight and strong.

Airframe manufactures composite materials based on structural cell cores (consisting of materials like aluminium and polycarbonate). Surface materials for Airframe's cored panels include Kevlar, carbon fibre, glass fibre, polyester and polycarbonate. By choosing the desired core material and appropriate surface (translucent or opaque), the designer can develop a vertical or horizontal structure addressing transparency, privacy, durability, UV resistance and acoustic qualities. Cored panels come in either 10.16 x 20.32 cm or 10.16 x 25.4 cm and generally are 1.91 cm thick.
These kinds of lightweight but strong composite materials were initially developed for use in the aircraft and naval industries.

70

LIGHT-WEIGHT TABLETOP

Composition
High-density wood fibreboard, cardboard

Properties
Completely recyclable, only half the weight of a solid-wood tabletop that can hold the same static load, suitable for a wide variety of finishes (veneer, high-pressure laminate, varnish, lacquer, linoleum, etc.), no supporting elements required to attach legs

Applications
Tabletops, doors

Contact
Wogg
Im Grund 16
Dättwil
CH-5405 Baden
Switzerland
T +41 (0)56 483 3700
F +41 (0)56 483 3719
info@wogg.ch
www.wogg.ch

Photo
Wogg's innovative tabletop is only half the weight of a comparable, solid-wood tabletop, but equally strong.

This lightweight tabletop is a patent-pending design developed and manufactured by Wogg. It is only half the weight of a comparable, solid-wood tabletop, but equally strong. Outer layers are made of a wood fibreboard whose relative density exceeds 1000 kg/m3, while the lightweight inner structure is made of a closed-cell cardboard honeycomb material with a density of 80 kg/m3. The innovative aspect lies in how the two are connected. Research and development topped two years, a period during which Wogg discovered how to unite the layers so tightly and solidly that the tabletop requires no internal supporting elements. Consequently, fixtures and fittings can be attached to any part of the tabletop. The material is suitable for various finishes, including veneers and coatings. Wogg has also developed an edge profile that can be securely attached to the tabletop; it has a soft, tactile, rubberised outer layer and a hard inner layer. In combination with the rounded shape of the basic design, this profile produces a durable tabletop with impact-absorbing edges. Designers can use the material to make objects that are manufactured and marketed exclusively by Wogg. To date, Wogg has no licensing contracts.

71

SANDWICH SHEET

Composition
Aluminium, polypropylene

Properties
Strong, combines high flexural stiffness and extreme lightness, produces a less metallic sound than steel sheet or aluminium, easy to recycle, reduces transport costs, provides X-ray protection

Applications
Automotive and transport industries (sandwich sheets or super-light panels with Hylite skin), architectural surfaces, office supplies (ring binders, photo albums, storage boxes)

Technical specifications
www.corusgroup-hylite.com/product_info/index.htm

Contact
Corus Hylite
PO Box 10000
NL-1970 CA IJmuiden
The Netherlands
T +31 (0)251 491 708
F +31 (0)251 471 051
www.corusgroup-hylite.com

Oosterhuis.nl
Essenburgsingel 94c
NL-3022 EG Rotterdam
The Netherlands
T +31 (0)10 244 7039
F +31 (0)10 244 7041
oosterhuis@oosterhuis.nl
www.oosterhuis.nl

Photo
Oosterhuis.nl designed a pavilion for the 2002 Dutch Floriade (Haarlemmermeer Polder, the Netherlands); the structure featured light-but-strong Hylite sandwich panels.
Photography by Oosterhuis.nl.

Hylite sandwich sheet consists of two layers of aluminium and a polypropylene interlayer. This featherweight composite material is simple to recycle, as its plastic core melts at a low temperature for easy removal. When used in the automotive industry, Hylite is a fuel-saving and thus an environmentally friendly solution. In the medical sector, it protects patients from exposure to unwanted X-rays.
Sandwich sheet can also be used as an architectural surface. The 'elastic skin' covering North Holland's interactive pavilion at the 2002 Dutch Floriade was made of Hylite sheet. Designed by Oosterhuis.nl, the futuristic structure (called The Web of North Holland) had a pentagonal interior wrapped in an ultra-streamlined shell: a space frame clad in curved Hylite triangles. The lightweight material produced a construction that swayed slightly on a windy day. Built in a workshop, each composite panel and curved surface was unique; the project exemplified mass customisation.

72

HONEYCOMB PAPERBOARD

Composition
Various types of paper, adhesive

Properties
Lightweight, strong (withstands heavy loads), easy to handle, easy to process by hand or machine, safe (no risk of damage to surrounding products), recyclable, compression-resistant, reduces transport costs, high energy absorption (10-16 kJ/kg), good price/performance ratio, simple waste management, moisture-absorbent (unsuitable for long-life applications)

Applications
Protective packaging for industrial transport, structural core material (automotive sandwich constructions), doors, furniture, exterior walls, partitions, whiteboards, display and exhibition construction

Contact
Besin International
PO Box 120
NL-3850 AC Ermelo
The Netherlands
T +31 (0)341 554 040
F +31 (0)341 554 200
info@besin.com
www.besin.com

Photo
BeeBoard consists of a honeycomb structure sandwiched between two layers of paper. The material is light, strong and inexpensive.

Honeycomb structures are light but strong. Layers of paper (or materials such as plastic or aluminium) are joined with staggered lines of glue. The stacked volumes are subsequently cut into strips. Thanks to the staggered application of glue, the result is a harmonica-like structure that resembles a honeycomb. BeeBoard is the brand name of a material made by applying a layer of paper to either side of a paper honeycomb structure. The material is strong, rigid, extremely lightweight and available in all sizes and thicknesses. Colour options are white and brown. The honeycomb core offers resistance to vertical compression unequalled by materials of comparable cost and weight. Because of its excellent capacity to distribute shock absorption over the area of impact, it protects products and people far better than polymer foams. BeeBoard is easy to process, cut, die cut and score; it can also be contoured. Variations in thickness and quality of paper, the size of the honeycomb cells and the number of stacked layers make the material suitable for a diversity of applications. In packaging, items can be protected and stabilised with a minimum of packaging material when honeycomb paperboard is provided with cavities and/or indentations designed to support a specific product.

73

STABILISED ALUMINIUM FOAM

Composition
Aluminium, particles of other metal

Properties
High strength-to-weight ratio,provides thermal and acoustic insulation, non-combustible, completely recyclable, versatile (bends when heated and is easy to cut and score)

Applications
Wall cladding, raised flooring, suspended ceilings, signs and exhibits, shelving, fixtures, furniture

Contact
Alusion (Cymat Corporation)
6320-2 Danville Road
Mississauga Ontario L5T 2L7
Canada
T +1 905 696 2419
F +1 905 696 9300
www.alusion.com

Photo
Stabilised aluminium foam combines the strength of aluminium with the lightness of foam.

Alusion is a strong, lightweight, completely recyclable panel of stabilised aluminium foam (SAF); the product combines the strength of aluminium with the lightness of foam. It first appeared in the automotive, aerospace and military industries in about 2000. Consisting of aluminium combined with particles of other metal, the alloy looks something like a metallic sponge. It appears to be far heavier than it is; the inner structure of each section is filled with thousands of air pockets, which make it surprisingly lightweight and a good thermal and acoustic insulator.
Alusion's capacity as a thermal insulator can be upgraded by added a thin layer of a nonconductive material such as ceramic.
Panels can be made up to 121.92 cm wide and 609.6 cm long; thickness varies from 1.27 to 6.35 cm. They come in two densities: the higher density is approximately 15 per cent aluminium and the lower about 10 per cent. Although Alusion is a closed-cell material, it has an open-cell finish that restricts sound transmission by up to 90 per cent. Available finishes include natural, open cell, glass coated, epoxy coated, coloured and translucent. The natural colour is a metallic shade of silver that can be powder coated or painted in any colour. Panels are easily cut and scored (on the back). Bending the foam requires a heating process similar to that used to bend glass. Bending does break the inner cells, however, considerably reducing the strength of the material. It is recommended only for aesthetic purposes or for use in conjunction with another material, such as an aluminium skin.

74

TENSIONED MEMBRANCE

Composition
Woven fibreglass, Teflon PTFE coating

Properties
Extremely versatile, highly durable (up to 25 years) in the most extreme climatic conditions, low-maintenance, optimum transmission of diffuse colour-correct light, conserves energy by reducing the need for artificial lighting

Applications
Roof construction, detached buildings, skylights, air-supported structures, umbrella-like shade structures

Technical specifications
www.birdair.com/birdair/standard/tech/index.html

Contact
Birdair
65 Lawrence Bell Drive
Amherst NY 14221
USA
T +1 716 633 9500
F +1 716 633 9850
sales@birdair.com
www.birdair.com

Photo
The Cargolifter Airship Hangar by SIAT Architekten & Ingenieure features a roof of tensioned membranes. Photography by Palladium.
Photo design by Barbara Burg and Oliver Schuh.

Sheerfill is a highly versatile architectural membrane that consists of a woven electrical-grade fibreglass substrate with a Teflon PTFE coating. This tensioned membrane transmits up to 20 per cent of daylight without the heat gain of traditional glazing. Shaded areas remain bright, yet cool, even on the hottest days. During the day the membranes provide a soft, diffuse translucence indoors, while appearing opaque when viewed from outside the building. At night, artificial interior lighting creates the exterior luminescence so characteristic of this product. Age does not alter the translucent quality of the membrane, and sunlight bleaches the material, thus preventing discoloration. Structures made of Sheerfill adapt to all climatic conditions, thanks to the chemically inert Teflon coating, which tolerates temperatures from -73°C to +232°C. Rain falling on the hydrophobic surface helps keep the material clean and fresh.
Applications last 20 years and more without any appreciable reduction in strength when measured against original design parameters.
The technology that preceded this product was developed in the 1950s for early-warning radar enclosures. The fabric structures used for that purpose satisfied the need for prefabricated, easy-to-erect shelters that could stand the extremes of a sub-polar climate.Tensioned membranes are used to construct roofs, detached buildings and skylights. By combining a variety of panel shapes, architects faced with complex aesthetic and functional challenges can create nearly any geometric configuration imaginable. Large-scale projects, such as London's Millennium Dome and the New Denver International Airport, prove that design solutions featuring tensioned membranes can be a low-cost alternative to traditional roofing and construction techniques.
The Millennium Dome, has a 320-m diameter for which 188,000 square metres of outer and inner fabric were used to cover the cable net.

75

MOULDABLE HONEYCOMB SHEET MATERIAL

Composition
Cardboard, coconut husks, polyester

Properties
Translucent, decorative, mouldable, available in various colours and thicknesses

Applications
Lighting solutions, ceiling panels, tables, doors, architectural components

Contact
Heideveld Polyester
Europaweg 24
NL-8181 BH Heerde
The Netherlands
T +31 (0)57 869 2058
F +31 (0)57 869 4651
info@heideveld-polyester.nl
www.heideveld-polyester.nl

Nuovopovero
487/40 Ratchaparob Road
Kweang Makkasan
Khet Ratchatevee 10400 Bangkok
Thailand
T/F +66 (0)2 375 6359
rudolfp@nuovopovero.com
www.nuovopovero.com

Photo
Translucent sheet material with a honeycomb core of cardboard and coconut husks coated in polyester can be used to make three-dimensional objects.

The core of this material – a honeycomb made of cardboard and coconut husks – is coated on both sides with a semi-transparent layer of coloured polyester. By varying the pressure and the amount of polyester resin, one can modify the appearance of the object being made. One result is a fluid, wavy surface that resembles snakeskin. Light gives the material a fascinatingly transparent, unguent glow. The brand name of the material is You See Through. It is available in various colours and degrees of transparency. A standard panel, uncoloured, measures 2600 x 1000 mm. But standard colours – black, red, blue and green – are also available. Clients ordering in excess of 500 m2 can choose from a palette that includes graphite, snow, ruby, indigo and sage. The manufacturer is also prepared to meet special requirements pertaining to fire safety, strength and UV-resistance.
The material is suitable for a wide range of applications. As a ceiling panel, it is an alternative for acoustic-ceiling-board and track-ceiling systems. Backlit ceiling panels create a particularly striking effect. Also available are three-dimensional varieties that can be used, for example, to create an undulating ceiling.

FRE
EFO
RM

INTRO

A major challenge facing architecture and design is the problem of how to make constructions lighter without making them weaker. Modern materials with a high strength-to-weight ratio are the solution. Most of these materials were developed in America for the aerospace industry and the United States Navy, where they are used to make light, strong, impact-resistant bodies and hulls for planes and ships.

Recently, honeycomb structures have also made their way into architecture. A number of companies have developed composite materials that feature a honeycomb structure of aluminium or cardboard, for example, sandwiched by transparent, translucent or opaque layers of substances such as glass, polymer, carbon fibre and fibreglass. Applications include doors, table pods, room dividers and flooring. Honeycomb structures combined with light can be used to create beautiful optical effects.

Equally lightweight, strong and rigid is a spongy material known as stabilised aluminium foam. It is used in the automotive industry, among others, as reinforcement for the chassis and as a shock absorber in bonnets, doors and boots. Two other obvious applications of this material are architectural components and furniture design.

Architects are experimenting with solid materials that are light in a figurative sense. Still in an early phase of development, translucent-transparent concrete resembles conventional concrete in all but appearance. Were such a product to appear on the market, the consequences for architecture would be enormous: designers would have the opportunity to replace windows with bearing walls that allow light to enter the building. Less high-tech, but already realised in the Netherlands, is a house made of sheets of glass glued together.

In addition to solid materials, today's market offers the designer super-strong, flexible fibres. A good example is Dyneema, a stronger-than-steel material used in the manufacture of canvas, bulletproof cockpit doors, helmets and impact-resistant tents. Special composite fabrics, such as Tyfo Fibrwrap, are used to wrap disintegrating and unstable sections of concrete structures like bridges and building foundations. This remedy reinforces the wrapped section and protects it from outside influences, including earthquakes. The fabric is impregnated with a special epoxy resin that not only makes it strong, but also causes the material to adhere to concrete.

The development of super fibres is still in the early stages. Scientists are currently studying the exact composition of what may be the strongest material on earth: the cobweb. As soon as industry is able to reproduce and mass-produce the strong filament spun by certain spiders, innovations in the fields of architecture and design will not be far behind.

76

STRETCH CEILINGS

Composition
Titanium-based, flexible vinyl sheeting

Properties
Elastic, recyclable, non-corrosive, waterproof, durable, self-extinguishing, easy to clean, enhances acoustic and insulation performance when used in conjunction with quilted materials

Applications
Vaulted ceilings, complex shapes, projection screens

Technical specifications
Video downloads via www.barrisol.com

Contact
Barrisol Normalu
Rue du Sipes
F-68680 Kembs
France
T +33 (0)3 8983 2020
F +33 (0)3 8948 4344
mail@barrisol.com
www.barrisol.com

Photo
Former design outfit The Fridge used stretch-fabric membranes for an installation at the Canadian Centre for Architecture (CCA) in Montreal. Photography by Michel Legendre.

Wall-to-wall stretch ceilings, which are made of a thin, flexible, fabric membrane – usually PVC – can cover spaces measuring hundreds and hundreds of square metres. The system consists of a custom-cut, stretch-fabric membrane held in place by semirigid PVC harpoons and a wall-mounted rail. The material is available in a variety of different colours and finishes. Perforated or translucent versions are used for lighting diffusers, projection screens and backlighting. Painting or printing techniques can be used to create interesting effects. Installation is clean and quick in both new-build and renovation projects. The material enables builders to bypass pipes or other conduits without resorting to complicated constructions. The system also makes it easy to cover structural elements or old ceilings, while providing accessibility when needed.
Its non-corrosive properties make it suitable for high-humidity projects, like pools and bathrooms.
The same material is suitable for wall coverings, light diffusers, floating panels, exhibitions and creative shapes.

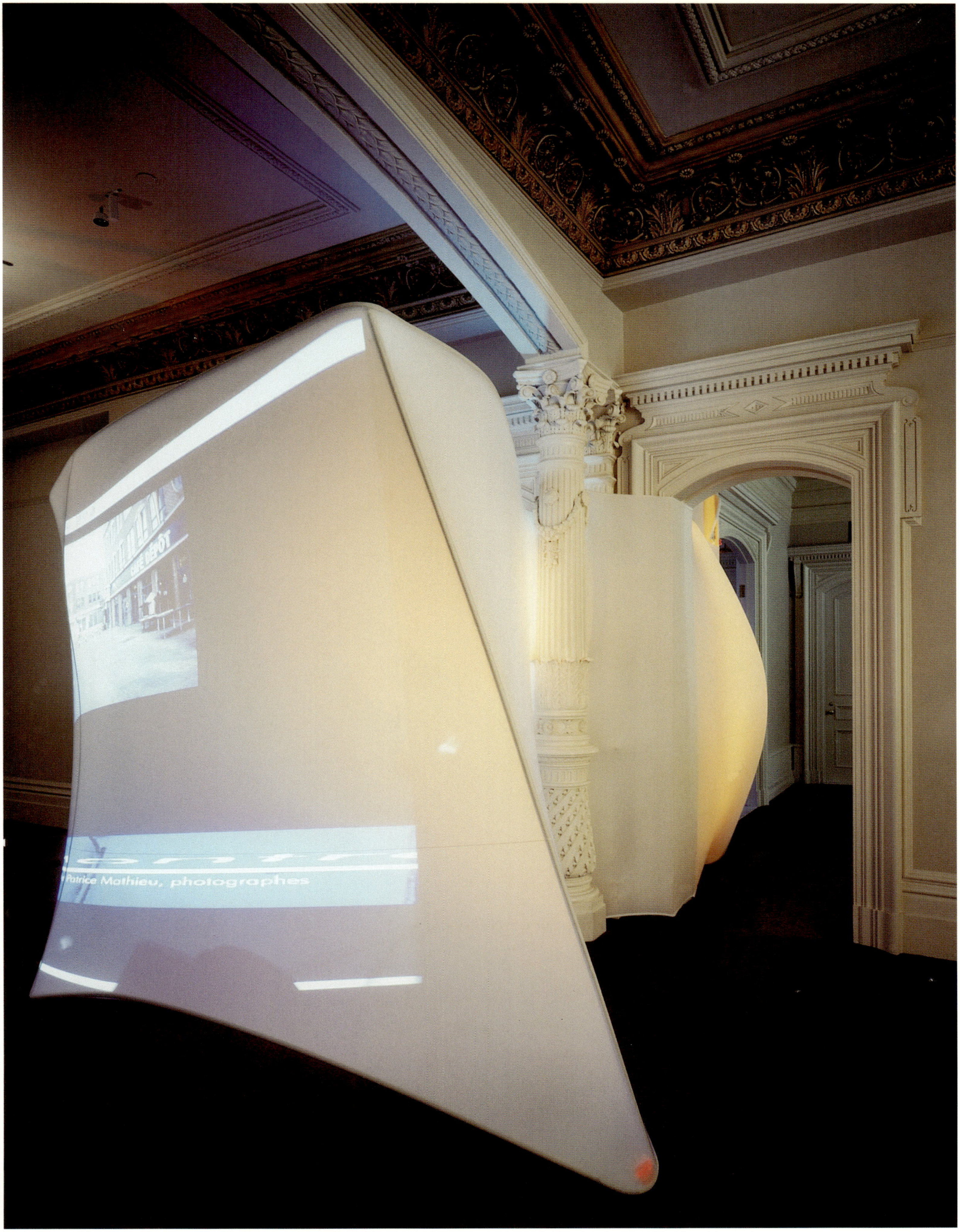
Patrice Mathieu, photographes

77

FOLDABLE POLY-PROPYLENE SHEETING

Composition
Polypropylene

Properties
Thin (3 mm thick), versatile, easy to manufacture, susceptible to scratches and imperfections, recyclable, nonflammable, chemical-resistant, available in different textures, suitable for screen printing

Applications
Furniture and other products

Contact
Polyline
Belgiëlei 4, bus 48
B-2018 Antwerp
Belgium
T +32 (0)32 185 397
F +32 (0)32 185 547
info@polyline.be
www.polyline.be

Horizon Plastics Company
PO Box 474
Cobourg Ontario K9A 4LI
Canada
T +1 905 372 2291
F +1 905 372 9397
horizon@eagle.ca

Photo
Polypropylene sheeting can be folded like paper.

Polypropylene is a material frequently used to manufacture packaging and products like lamp reflectors and home and office accessories (storage bins, file folders). Moulded or thermoformed, this thin plastic sheeting is suitable for many different finishes (including screen printing).
Belgian design agency Polyline has developed an alternative manufacturing and design method for polypropylene. The firm's Folder chair (40 x 40 x 80 cm) consists of a 3-mm-thick polypropylene sheet that is laser-cut, scored and folded to create a seating unit. Invisible snap-on fasteners provide the chair with stability. Thanks to its design and the mat surface of the material, the chair resembles an object made of white origami paper.

78

STEREO LITHO-GRAPHY

Composition
Epoxy-based photopolymer

Properties
Strong, rigid, impact-resistant, photosensitive, low colour, alternative for moulding and forming, recycles industrial waste, high level of design freedom, small production runs, enables user to build models early in design process, end result nearly replicates original design, high clarity, superior surface finish, withstands threaded holes, screws and press-fit bearings without cracking

Applications
See-through models and housings, transparent designer objects in small series

Contact
DSM Somos
2 Penn's Way
New Castle DE 19720
USA
T +1 302 328 5435
F +1 302 328 5693
americas@dsmsomos.info
europe@dsmsomos.info
www.dsmsomos.com

Materialise
Technologielaan 15
B-3001 Leuven
Belgium
T +32 (0)16 396 611
F +32 (0)16 396 600
software@materialise.be
prototype@materialise.be
www.materialise.be

Photo
Using WaterClear, a liquid photopolymer, designer Marcel Wanders and manufacturer Materialise created a tiara that expresses the delicacy of water. Photography by DSM Somos.

Stereo lithography is a layer-additive, rapid-prototyping process featuring the use of photopolymer liquid resins that solidify when exposed to UV light. A software program transfers a 3-D CAD model into an electronic file for stereo lithography machines, composing the information into thin cross sections or layers. A laser beam then traces each layer onto the surface of a vat of photopolymer resin, building the part in repeated layers until a solid replica of the original CAD model is completed. Stereo lithography is often the process of choice when the designer wants an attractive and accurate model with a fine surface finish. The primary drawback of this technology lies in the photosensitive nature of the materials used, which may change after prolonged exposure to UV light and/or other environmental conditions.
WaterClear 10120, a product manufactured by DSM Somos, is the first liquid photopolymer that has both strength and optical clarity. A composite material with diverse properties of interest to engineers, this resin boasts the flexural strength and modulus of polycarbonate, the notched Izod impact strength of Nylon 66 and the tensile strength of ABS. The resin can be used to build see-through models for the purpose of evaluating product assemblies. This application includes engine components, power tools, light pipes, bottles, lenses and any project that involves visualising the flow of liquids or gases. Multiple iterations of components realised with stereo lithography can be made as the design evolves. Objects can be dyed to add colour to the result.
Marcel Wanders and his team used WaterClear for the prototype of a tiara designed for Dutch royalty. Inspired by nature, Wanders created a delicate, crystalline diadem that evokes an image of water, the element so vital to Dutch culture. His concept can be traced to a splash of water – magnificent, natural, graceful and transparent.

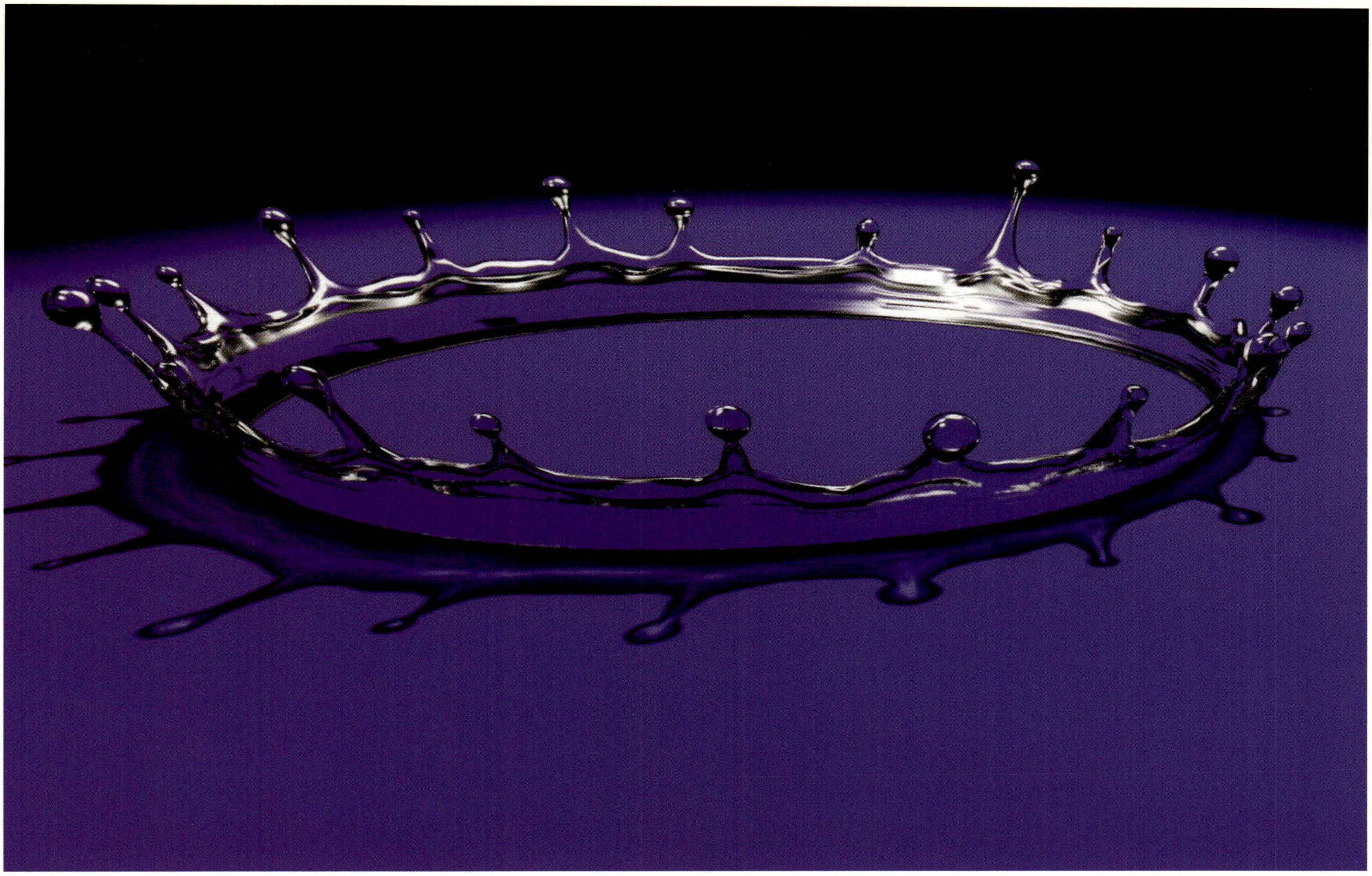

79

COCOON SPRAY

Composition
Elastic PVC fibre

Properties
Sprayable, elastic, impenetrable, shrinks after application

Applications
Wrapping objects, creating skins for suspension structures

Contact
Jurgen Bey
Passerelstraat 44a
NL-3023 ZD Rotterdam
The Netherlands
T +31 (0)10 425 8792
bey@luna.nl

Droog Design
Rusland 3
NL-1012 CK Amsterdam
The Netherlands
T +31 (0)20 626 9809
F +31 (0)20 638 8828
info@droogdesign.nl
www.droogdesign.nl

Photo
In a project for Droog Design, Jurgen Bey and Jan Konings used cocoon spray to make a new object out of old pieces of furniture. Photography by Bob Goedewagen.

Described as a cross between textile and chewing gum, cocoon spray is an excellent material for filling gaps. The structural use of such a material dates back to the late 1950s, when a couple of tubular-steel structures wrapped in strips of cloth and clad in a skin of cocoon spray were erected at the Illinois Institute of Technology. John Zerning uses cocoon spray as a mould-forming technique for the skins of suspension structures. The United States Air Force has used the technology to encase aircraft in a protective elastic skin for storage purposes. Dutch designers Jurgen Bey and Jan Konings, together with Droog Design, have used the cocoon-spray technique to create new items of furniture. Bey and Konings sprayed a couple of pieces of old wooden furniture with the material to create an object with an entirely new look. The sprayed coating shrinks, encasing the skeleton in an elastic skin. The technique works so well because all elements and all intermediate spaces are covered by a single skin.

80

FABRIC-LAYERED FOAM

Composition
Polyethylene foam and fabric

Properties
Flexible, soft-textured, lightweight, nonslip, shock-resistant, easy to clean, sound-absorbent, provides thermal insulation, suitable for vacuum forming

Applications
Furniture, tiles, floor mats, room dividers, wall coverings

Contact
Emmy Blok
Verwerstraat 82
NL-5612 EE Eindhoven
The Netherlands
T +31 (0)6 5516 2932
to@emmyblok.myweb.nl

Alveo
Bahnhofstrasse 7
CH-6002 Lucerne
Switzerland
T +41 (0)41 228 9292
F +41 (0)41 228 9200
info@alveo.com
www.alveo.com

Project Total Coating
Acaciastraat 1
NL-5802 EK Venray
The Netherlands
T +31 (0)478 511 500
F +31 (0)478 510 060
info@ptc.nl
www.ptc.nl

Photo
Dutch designer Emmy Blok upgrades polyethylene foam by adding a layer of fabric and vacuum forming the composite to give it a textured, patterned surface.

Emmy Block, a student at The Design Academy in Eindhoven, based her graduation project on a study of how to make polyethylene (PE) more suitable for use in interior design. One possibility is to apply a layer of fabric to PE foam. After the foam is heated to a temperature that allows the fabric to adhere to it, the composite is vacuum formed to give the material a flexible, textured surface with a 'soft' look.
Because the properties of the material are so varied, applications are countless. Examples include upholstery for furniture and cushions (flexible, soft), tiles and bathroom mats (easy to clean, soft, nonslip), and room dividers or 3-D wall coverings for contract furnishing (insulating, sound-absorbent, attractive).

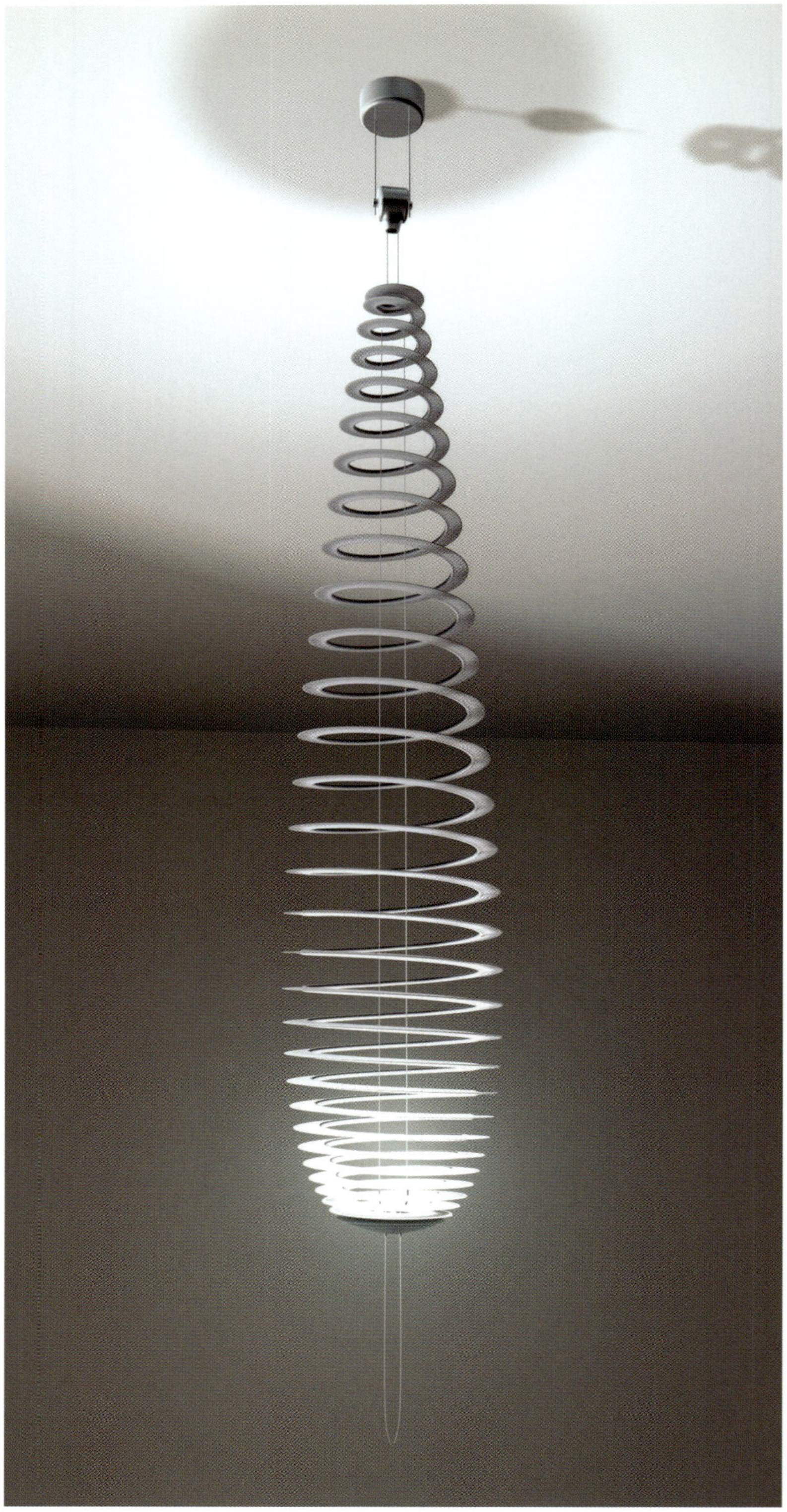

81

SELECTIVE LASER SINTERING

Composition
Polyamide powder

Properties
Alternative for moulding and forming, recycles industrial waste, high level of design freedom, small production runs, end result nearly replicates original design, rough surface, high mechanical and thermal resistance, long exposure to UV light and other environmental conditions may produce changes in the material

Applications
Hollow products with other products inside, moulds, limited-series designer objects

Contact
Materialise
Technologielaan 15
B-3001 Leuven
Belgium
T +32 (0)16 396 611
F +32 (0)16 396 600
software@materialise.be
prototype@materialise.be
www.materialise.be

Ron Arad Associates
62 Chalk Farm Road
London NW1 8AN
UK
T +44 (0)20 7284 4963
F +44 (0)20 7379 0499
info@ronarad.com
www.ronarad.com

Photo
Thanks to selective laser sintering, objects can be grown in a tank with the use of computer-controlled laser beams. Shown are lamps from the Not Made by Hand, Not Made in China collection designed by Ron Arad.

Selective laser sintering (SLS) involves heating thermoplastic powder to create products. A laser beam – controlled by CAD data from a 3-D computer model – heats layer by layer of powder, selectively fusing layers together as desired. The sintering process is repeated until the product is finished. This computer-controlled technique turns out virtually exact reproductions of the original design.
The powder normally used is a type of polyamide that is not too hard and not too soft. The addition of fibreglass leads to a harder product. The advantage of SLS over moulding and forming is its capacity to create highly complex homogeneous components. An extra hole for removing residual powder is essential, however. The advantage of SLS over stereolithography is that the former requires no supporting struts.
The technology stems from military research into how to repair damaged space stations without making costly expeditions to replace a small number of broken components. The possibility of making components from metallic powder (a material abundantly present in the atmosphere and on planets) without using moulds or large-scale machinery led researchers to the computer-controlled laser. Belgian firm Materialise uses the same technology to make replicas of bones, with data taken from medical scans. Materialise manufactured Ron Arad's Not Made by Hand, Not Made in China collection, for example. These lamps are made of DuraForm, a polyamide powder. Arad sent Materialise animated computer models of leaping vases, lamps and bowls. Such animations can be freeze-framed at any point; the resulting objects duplicate a 'frozen' image capable of being expanded or compressed.
All objects were grown in a tank with the use of computer-controlled laser beams. The technique opens the way for the mass production of countless similar, but always slightly different, items.

82

METAL INJECTION MOULDING

Composition
Metal powder (316L stainless steel or pure titanium: grade 4)

Properties
Suitable for complex shapes, series production (from a few thousand to hundreds of thousands of pieces) and a variety of standard finishes; can be engraved; very good surface quality

Applications
Watch clasps, customised buckles, hinges and other eyewear components, cams

Contact
Comotec
Fort des Rousses - BP 42
F-39220 Les Rousses
France
T +33 (0)3 8460 5600
F +33 (0)3 8460 5636
comotec@comotec.com
www.comotec.com

Photo
Metal injection moulding makes it possible to cast metals like stainless steel and titanium in complex moulds to create articles with a highly attractive finish.

Metal injection moulding (MIM) makes it possible to cast metals like stainless steel and titanium in complex moulds to create articles with a highly attractive finish. It is a three-stage process that begins by mixing metal powder (60 per cent) with a thermoplastic material (40 per cent) like polyacetal, a natural resin. The mixture is injected into a mould. The plastic liquefies at a temperature of 150°C and disperses the metal powder (which reaches its melting point at a higher temperature) throughout the mould. The model is reheated to a temperature of 200°C, a gas is added, and the result is a chemical reaction that converts the plastic into formaldehyde. What remains is a fragile, porous model: a rather spongy object composed of metal powder. The next step is to sinter the model at 1200°C to make all the particles stick together.
A shrinkage factor of 16 per cent means that all pores are filled up.
A disadvantage of this technology is that it can be used only to make objects smaller than a wristwatch. This is due to the shrinkage factor, as well as to the duration of the process, which makes it a costly operation. In most cases, components are between 0.4 and 8.0 mm thick and from 0.1 to 100 g, with typical dimensional tolerances of ±0.3 per cent. The possibility does exist, of course, to combine several components in a single piece. Engraved texts, either raised or recessed, can be integrated into the injection mould (0.25 mm deep).

2

FINISHINGTOUCH

INTRO

The skin of products, interiors and even buildings is a matter of greater interest than ever before. After all, the surface of an object or a space – even when finished with inexpensive materials – represents a chance to upgrade the most mediocre design. In experimenting with finishing techniques, manufacturers and designers often find inspiration in disciplines other than their own.

Take aromatic inks and paints, for instance. Although no strangers to fashion and graphics, they are virtually unknown in architectural, product and interior design. It doesn't take much imagination to come up with suitable applications, however. What about impregnating the paint used on garden furniture with an odour repellent to mosquitoes? Or upholstering a sofa in a fabric that releases a clean fragrance for a programmable period of time? The insulating ceramic coating that Klein Dytham architecture applied to a steel garage roof was originally developed for the aerospace industry.

The right finishing touch can tap a new target group or respond to a changing market. Dalsouple's magnetic rubber tiles, which are installed directly on a metal subfloor, take advantage of the growing number of office floors equipped with metal flooring systems that lend access to electrical wires and cables. When used with such systems, magnetic tiles are a good alternative for removable products like carpet tiles and various types of wall-to-wall flooring.

Manufacturers continue to invest in easy-to-clean materials for spaces demanding a high standard of hygiene. Examples are Trespa Virtuon, a strong, nonporous sheet material; and Bonar Floors' Flotex, a floor covering with a waterproof backing and a virtually impenetrable pile structure.

'Made to measure' skin is another intriguing concept. A reaction to mass production is the finishing technique that allows for the realisation of small, unique production runs. Royal Tichelaar Makkum employs a special technique to imprint photographic images on glazed tiles. Abet relies on a digital, four-colour printing procedure to apply scanned computer images directly to laminate paper or thin sheets of aluminium. Designers email their designs to the company and the procedure is completed within hours, without the need for physical drawings or filmed images. It's a big step on the path to individualised interiors and furnishings.

VF0804
VF1904

VFAA04
VF1963

83

3-D PATTERNED SHEETS

Composition
Polyvinyl chloride (PVC)

Properties
Translucent or opaque, rigid or flexible, easy to work with, has a three-dimensional effect

Applications
Laminates, floor tiles, furniture, lampshades, displays, shoes

Contact
Mazzucchelli 1849
Via Santino e Pompeo
Mazzucchelli 7
I-21043 Castiglione Olona (VA)
Italy
T +39 03 3182 6111
F +39 03 3182 6213
direzionegenerale@
mazzucchelli1849.it
www.mazzucchelli1849.it

Photo
The motif on 3-D patterned PVC sheets is not superficial. It is completely embedded in the material, giving the product a surprising three-dimensional effect.

Marketed as Sicobloc, these PVC sheets have a three-dimensional pattern embedded right in the product. A computer-controlled process produces large blocks of PVC.
The motifs, however, are created by hand. A curing process involving heat and pressure produces a big block of PVC that is marked with the pattern from one side to the other. Sheets are 'shaved' from this block, one at a time. They are flexible or rigid, translucent or opaque, depending on thickness (a minimum of 0.2 mm). Various colours and motifs are available. Sheets can be used as they are or modified by means of polishing, embossing or printing. They can be laminated to other sheets of rigid plastic (PVC or acrylic) and to wood panels. Both flexible and rigid sheets can be cut with conventional tools. They can be glued and printed with PVC-compatible glues and inks.
The flexible sheets are suitable for welding, and the rigid sheets can be thermoformed.

84

WATER-PROOF CARPET

Composition
Polyamide fibres, fibreglass, vinyl

Properties
Waterproof, sound-absorbent, easy to install, nonslip, stain-resistant, antistatic, retains original dimensions

Applications
Public facilities such as hospitals, schools, hotels, airports and shops

Technical specifications
www.bonarfloors.com/flotex

Contact
Bonar Floors
High Holborn Road
Ripley
Derbyshire DE5 3NT
UK
T +44 (0)1773 744 121
F +44 (0)1773 744 142
bonarfloors.uk@lowandbonar.com
www.bonarfloors.com

Photo
Flotex floor covering has a waterproof backing, which means it can be cleaned with water or other liquid cleaning agents.

Flotex, a carpet suitable for contract furnishing, has a waterproof backing that tolerates intensive cleaning with water or other liquid cleaning agents. Because moisture cannot penetrate this resilient backing (which contains vinyl), the carpet resists the development of bacteria and mould. The specially designed pile of this floor covering makes it more hygienic than a softer carpet. The polyamide fibres of the surface layer are molecularly and electrostatically bonded to the fibreglass-reinforced backing, resulting in a highly durable product. The flocked carpet boasts a pile density of 80 million fibres per square metre. Because this dense forest of fibres stands upright, most dirt remains on the surface, where it can be vacuumed up easily. Thanks to the sturdy fibreglass layer between pile and backing, the flooring does not stretch or shrink, but retains its original dimensions. This antistatic product has no adverse effect on computers.

85

DROP TILE

Composition
Glass, ceramic

Properties
Frostproof, nonslip, produces massaging effect

Applications
Walls and floors (indoors and out)

Contact
Royal Tichelaar Makkum
PO Box 1
NL-8754 ZN Makkum
The Netherlands
T +31 (0)515 231 341
F +31 (0)515 232 555
info@tichelaar.nl
www.tichelaar.nl

Erik Jan Kwakkel
Klarendalseweg 532
NL-6822 GZ Arnhem
The Netherlands
T +31 (0)26 442 1896
F +31 (0)26 389 2525
kwakkel@knoware.nl

Arnout Visser
Alexanderstraat 33
NL-6812 BC Arnhem
The Netherlands
T +31 (0)26 442 9046
F +31 (0)26 351 4812

Photo
Glass globules adorn the surface of these ceramic Drop Tiles.

Glass and ceramic normally have an aversion to each other. Dutch designers Erik Jan Kwakkel and Arnout Visser worked with Royal Tichelaar Makkum for months to find a type of glass that would adhere to ceramic. The result is Drop Tile, a product whose surface appears to be covered with drops of liquid. Before these tiles go into the kiln, pieces of glass are applied to them by hand. During firing, the glass liquefies to form globules that adhere to the ceramic tiles during the cooling process. Each tile is unique. Drop Tiles have a massaging effect, are nonslip and are suitable for both floor and wall application. The product was launched in 1997 as part of Droog Design's Dry Bathing project.

86

AROMATIC INK

Composition
Perfumed capsules, water, binder

Properties
Scent released by scratching or rubbing, milk-white paste, shelf life of six months

Applications
Printing, dyeing (in combination with binder and fixative), heat transference

Contact
Matsui International Company
1501 West 178th Street
Gardena CA 90248
USA
T +1 310 767 7812
F +1 310 767 7836
info@matsui-color.com
www.matsui-color.com

Photo
Prior to application aromatic ink is a milk-white paste, but the end result is colourless.

Aromatic ink is a dispersing paste in which various kinds of perfume are compounded stably as well as in high concentration through a special technology. The desired essence is embedded in microcapsules that are combined with a dispersing agent. The result is a milk-white paste that becomes colourless after application. Aromatic ink is a relatively durable material that withstands laundering and other sources of heat for several years. It can be screen printed onto a variety of fabrics, including cotton, polyester and nylon.

87

COPPER-PLATED FABRIC

Composition
Woven or nonwoven fabric, copper plating

Properties
Extremely light, air-permeable, provides high levels of conductivity and shielding effectiveness, withstands folding and stretching without losing conductivity, tolerates up to 80 per cent humidity (after application), features anti-corrosion coating

Applications
Spaces that house sensitive equipment (computer centres, R&D labs, intensive-care units, neurology and cardiology units)

Contact
Schlegel
Rochesterlaan 4
B-8470 Gistel
Belgium
T +32 (0)59 270 300
F +32 (0)59 270 345
isowave@schlegel.be
www.schlegel.be

Photo
Copper-plated fabrics provide flexible, cost-efficient, electromagnetic safety for health-care and computer facilities.

Electromagnetic interference poses a serious threat to sensitive electronic equipment of the kind found in computer rooms, hospitals and laboratories. Until recently, the only way to provide electromagnetic safety was to shield such spaces with expensive panelling made of stainless steel or zinc-plated mild steel. The copper-plated fabric known as Isowave forms the basis of a flexible, cost-efficient shielding system that adapts to the shape of any room, making the material ideal for both new-build and renovation projects. Isowave can be applied to walls, ceilings and floors. It occupies a minimum of space, can be applied like wallpaper, and is compatible with most glues, paints and decorative materials. It can be finished with practically any floor or wall covering. Custom-made shielding doors, window blinds and a full range of complementary solutions are available.

88

MAGNETIC TILE

Composition
Rubber, magnetic backing

Properties
Hygienic, soft, flexible, sound- and impact-absorbent, nonslip, antistatic, (cigarette) burn-resistant

Applications
Metal subfloors (office environments) and other metal surfaces (for decorative and/or protective purposes)

Contact
Dalsouple
PO Box 140
Bridgwater TA5 1HT
UK
T +44 (0)1984 667 233
F +44 (0)1984 667 366
pr@dalsouple.com
www.dalsouple.com

Photo
Magnetic rubber tiles can easily be attached to steel surfaces.

Inspiration for a magnetic tile came from the growth in access flooring systems, as more and more contemporary buildings have access floors fitted during new-build or refurbishment projects. Dalsouple has developed a resilient rubber tile with a magnetic backing, a product ideal for use with metal subfloors accommodating electrical wires and cables that require accessibility. The magnetic force of this product is strong enough to create a stable walking surface with no slippage or shifting of tiles. For access to the subfloor, tiles are removed and replaced (as often as necessary). Magnetic tiles form a resilient alternative to conventional tiles and floor coverings. Dalsouple's magnetic tiles are available in 60 colours and a wide range of textures.

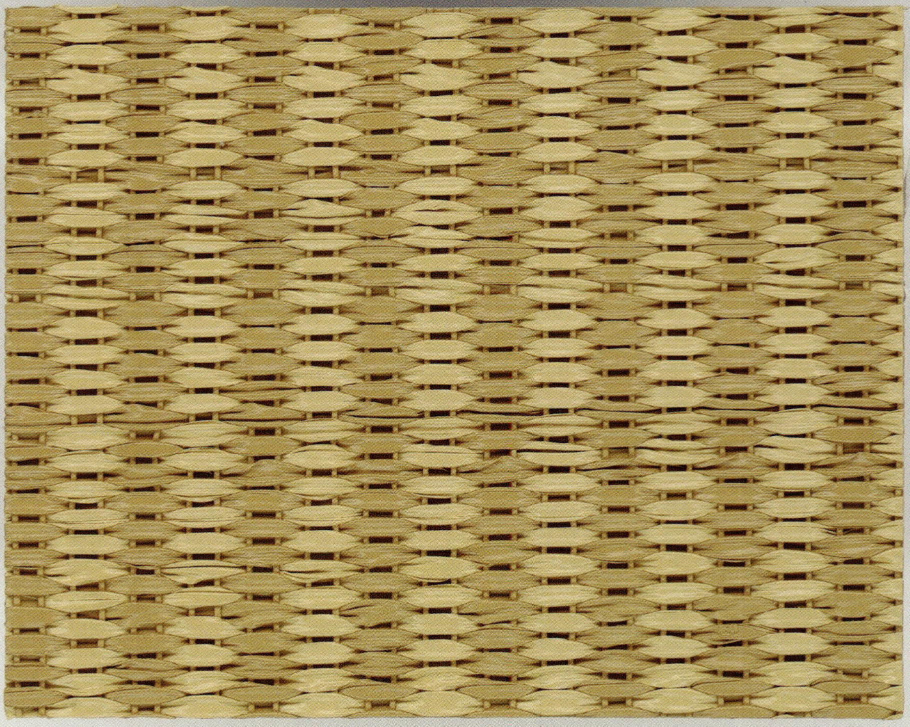

89

WOVEN VINYL FLOORING

Composition
Vinyl, polyester, fibreglass

Properties
Stain- and scratch-resistant, sound-absorbent, durable, colourfast, waterproof, low-maintenance, low operating costs, easy to clean

Applications
Public areas (indoors and out)

Contact
Bolon
PO Box 73
Vist Industriomrade
SE-523 22 Ulricehamn
Sweden
T +46 (0)321 530 400
F +46 (0)321 530 450
info@bolon.se
www.bolon.se

Photo
Woven vinyl flooring looks like a product made of natural materials, but it has the characteristics of a synthetic surface.

Durability and a natural look are the main characteristics of this woven vinyl flooring with a vinyl-and-fibreglass backing. The woven layer of this stain- and noise-resistant material is about 2 mm thick; together with the backing, the flooring is about 2.5 mm thick. Because the floor covering requires no special type of maintenance, operating costs are low. Dirt is hard to see on the special woven structure of this sound-absorbent surface, which cannot be permanently stained by either wine or grease. Application is quick and simple. Joints are invisible after installation. Sunlight has no effect on the colour. The material can be applied to access flooring systems that accommodate heating equipment. Signs and furnishings leave no marks; office chairs roll smoothly over the surface without scratching it.

90

DURABLE WALL COVERING

Composition
Prepegs (cellulose fibres and resins) with surface layers of impregnated kraft paper and resins

Properties
Durable, colourfast, eco-friendly, scratch- wear- and impact-resistant, easy to clean, easy to machine, tolerates most cleaning agents and disinfectants, provides good acoustics, has damage-resistant edges

Applications
Wall cladding, bumper rails, locker systems, sanitary facilities

Contact
Trespa International
PO Box 110
NL-6000 AC Weert
The Netherlands
T +31 (0)495 458 850
F +31 (0)495 540 535
infonederland@trespa.com
www.trespa.com

Photo
This durable wall covering has an impermeable surface comparable to that of synthetic flooring.

Trespa Virtuon is an interior wall composite comparable to a floor covering in terms of maintenance. Flat panels based on thermosetting resins are homogeneously reinforced with cellulose fibres and manufactured under high pressure at a high temperature. The basic composition resembles that of natural hardwood; the two materials react similarly to fire. Their machinability is comparable as well. Virtuon panels, however, have an integrated, decorative surface created with pigmented resins.
The surface consists of an impregnated kraft-paper substrate and a two-layer urethane-acrylic resin coating; the top layer is clear, and the area closest to the substrate is coloured. The core of the panels consists of pre-compressed fibre mats (prepegs) made of softwood fibres and thermosetting phenolic resin in a dry-forming process.
The final stage of production is panel pressing. The semi-finished products for both core and decorative surface are brought together in press packages and subjected to high pressure and high temperature (±150°C). During this process the reactive resins are completely and irreversibly cured. Resin molecules are bound to the surface during curing, leaving no pores in a product that satisfies the highest demands of hygiene, cleanability and moisture resistance.
It prevents the penetration of dirt and dyes, repels water and stains, and prevents damage from cleaning agents used to remove graffiti, calcium deposits and other undesirable substances. The warm look and tactile surface of this composite make it suitable for interior applications like toilet facilities, operating theatres and swimming pools.

91

DRY-ERASABLE WRITING SURFACE

Composition
Polyester fabric, vinyl coating

Properties
Flexible, smooth, suitable for standard dry-erase markers, easy to install, scratch- and fire-resistant

Applications
Flat or curved walls (offices, classrooms, conference rooms, daycare and health-care facilities)

Technical specifications
www.memerase.com/physprop_table.htm

Contact
Muraspec
74-78 Wood Lane End
Hemel Hempstead
Hertfordshire HP2 4RF
UK
T +44 (0)870 511 7118
F +44 (0)870 532 9020
customerservices@muraspec.com
www.muraspec.com

Photo
Dry-erasable wall covering can be written on with standard dry-erase markers, cleaned and reused ad infinitum.

Marketed as MemErase, this product is a flexible, vinyl-coated, polyester material that requires a heavy-duty, clay-based wallpaper adhesive for application. The result is a surface suitable for standard dry-erase markers. MemErase features a durable coating containing a patented release agent; the coating is applied to a fabric-backed vinyl. The product eliminates the discoloration and peeling that often occurs with laminated dry-erase material.
The flexible material can convert any wall space, flat or curved, into a durable dry-wipe surface. Hanging the panels horizontally creates a maximum usable surface and minimises ink bleed where panels join together. A gentle detergent and warm water are recommended for additional cleaning. A range of pastel colours complements the standard white version, and a white surface with a faint geometric grid pattern is available to aid graph plotting.

92

FUNCTIONAL, CONSTRUCTION AND KITCHEN TILES

Composition
Glazed ceramic

Properties
Waterproof, white, surface relief

Applications
Walls and floors of bathrooms and kitchens

Contact
Droog Design
Rusland 3
NL-1012 CK Amsterdam
The Netherlands
T +31 (0)20 626 9809
F +31 (0)20 638 8828
info@droogdesign.nl
www.droogdesign.nl

Erik Jan Kwakkel
Klarendalseweg 532
NL-6822 GZ Arnhem
The Netherlands
T +31 (0)26 442 1896
F +31 (0)26 389 2525
kwakkel@knoware.nl

Photo
Integrated into the design of the Functional Tile are options such as towel hook and toilet-paper holder.

As part of Droog Design's Dry Bathing project, Erik Jan Kwakkel, Peter van der Jagt and Arnout Visser developed a series of Functional Tiles for the bathroom. They based their 1997 design on standard 15-x-15-cm tiles, a size found in nearly every new-build home in Holland. Accompanying their design are options such as an integrated towel hook, toilet-paper holder and small medicine chest. The initial series provided users with flat tiles for two-dimensional bathroom walls. A later addition was a series of Construction Tiles, some of which have convex or concave surfaces, allowing them to be combined with Functional Tiles to create various sculptural effects. Another version of the Functional Tile is the aptly named Kitchen Tile, which requires no further description.

0
10
20
30
40
50

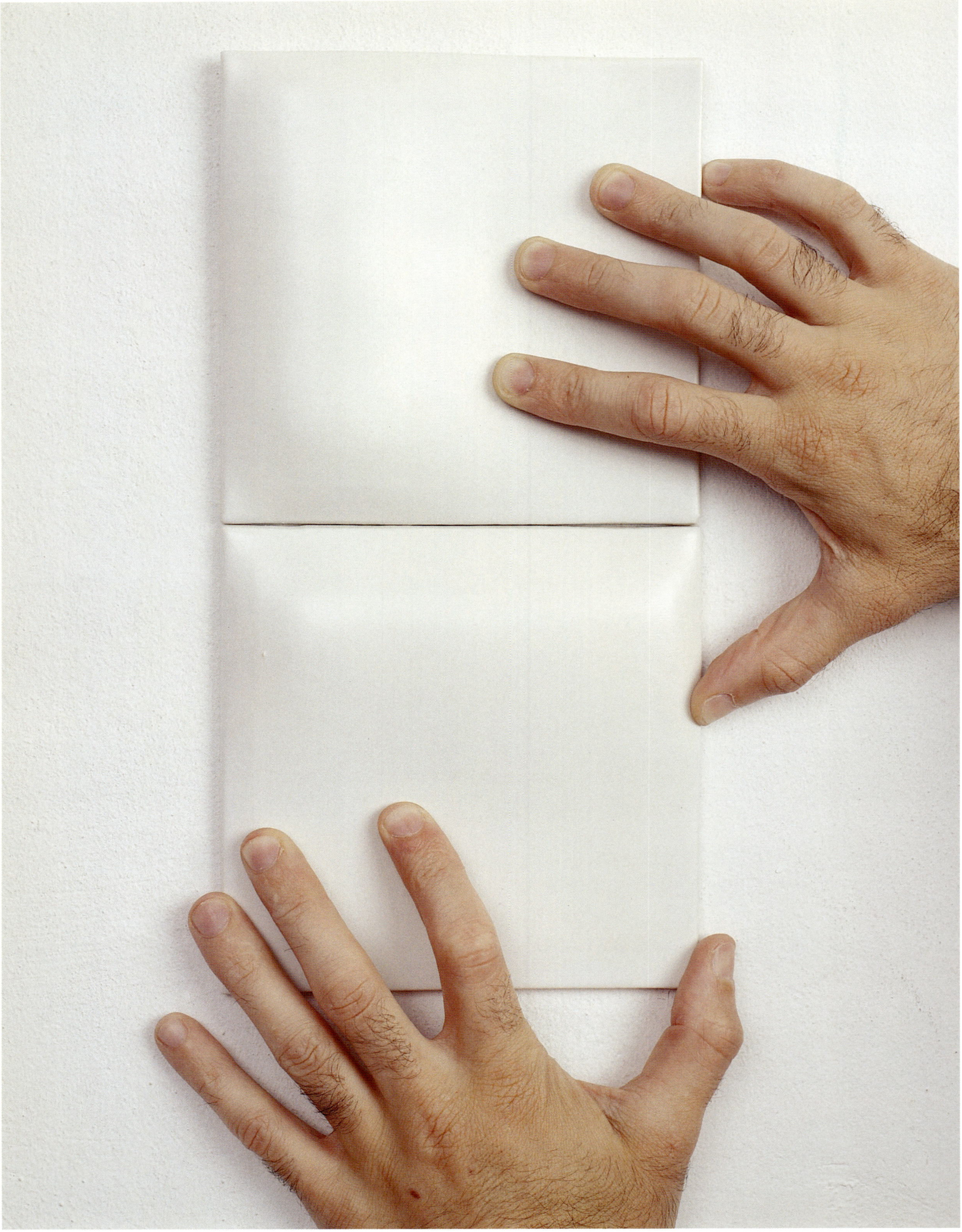

93

RELIEF TILES

Composition
Glazed ceramic

Properties
Tactile, features high relief, has a white mat glaze

Applications
Walls in bathrooms and similar environments

Contact
Baukje Trenning
F. Petterbaan 9
NL-1019 JT Amsterdam
The Netherlands
T +31 (0)20 694 6899
F +31 (0)20 419 4654
baukje@trenning.demon.nl

Royal Tichelaar Makkum
PO Box 1
NL-8754 ZN Makkum
The Netherlands
T +31 (0)515 231 341
F +31 (0)515 232 555
info@tichelaar.nl
www.tichelaar.nl

Photo
Tactile – a series of ceramic tiles designed by Baukje Trenning – displays an exceptionally high relief.

Dutch designer Baukje Trenning has created a series of 15-x-15-cm ceramic wall tiles in exceptionally high relief. In some cases she presses thumb or fist into the soft clay; other tiles are cut, gouged or pierced. Because the manufacturer of her designs is still equipped for manual production, the relief on Trenning's tiles can be as deep as 12 mm. After baking and glazing, the result is a white tile with a soft look that asks to be touched. This sensory invitation inspired the designer to call the tile Tactile. A wall of these tiles is a rhythmic surface and an animated show of light and shadow.

94

WOVEN HARD SURFACE

Composition
Polyester resin, polyethylene textile

Properties
Hard, durable, translucent or opaque, easy to clean, suitable for sawing and bending (by machine)

Applications
Tables, carts, doors, shelving and other types of furniture

Contact
Carnegie RVC
110 North Centre Avenue
Rockville Centre NY 11570
USA
T +1 516 678 6770
F +1 516 678 6848
mail@carnegiefabrics.com
www.carnegiefabrics.com
www.xorel.com

Photo
Xorel is a family of durable, easy-to-clean textile products for walls, panels and upholstery.

Thermofusing PETG (a polyester resin) with textile results in a hard, tactile surface that is durable, easy to clean and eco-friendly; it contains no chlorine or plasticisers. Marketed as Xorel, the material combines the colours, patterns and textures of a woven textile with the strength and flexibility of a rigid material. Patterns and colours are vibrant, and depending on the pattern chosen, the material is either translucent or opaque. The surface can be embossed or textured. The material itself can be drilled, cut, bent, tapped into, routed or sawed in much the same way as wood.
It can be mechanically bent as well as draped into forms and heated, creating design possibilities that are as flexible as a designer's imagination.

95

PHOTO TILES

Composition
Glazed ceramic

Properties
Durable, solid, suitable for all images

Applications
Walls and floors (indoors and out)

Contact
Royal Tichelaar Makkum
PO Box 1
NL-8754 ZN Makkum
The Netherlands
T +31 (0)515 231 341
F +31 (0)515 232 555
info@tichelaar.nl
www.tichelaar.nl

Photo
Shown are two examples of photographic images on tile.

A special transfer technique makes it possible to permanently imprint a photographic image on a tile. The process begins with a screen-printing technique, which translates the colours of the photo into glazes. The glazes are applied to the tile, the tile is fired and the resulting object bears an exact copy of the original photo. Applications are endless.

96

HIGH-PRESSURE LAMINATE DIGITAL PRINT

Composition
Print on laminated paper or aluminium sheet

Properties
Digital, cheaper and faster than related manufacturing methods, high level of design freedom, no minimal production runs, end result nearly replicates original design

Applications
Building façades (panels), interior finishes, furniture

Contact
Abet Laminati
Viale Industria 21
I-12042 Bra
Italy
T +39 0172 419 111
F +39 0172 431 571
abet@abet-laminati.it
www.abet-laminati.it

Photo
Using the digital-printing technology, manufacturers can reproduce virtually any image on high-pressure laminate. Dumoffice, a group of designers inspired by the phenomenon of the automobile, applied the technology to the photograph pictured here. Photography by Oof Verschuuren.

The core of high-pressure laminate (HPL) consists of kraft paper impregnated with phenolic resin, while the surface comprises printed or coloured decor paper impregnated with pure melamine resin. Printed decors require a transparent overlay to protect the print from abrasion. Thanks to the digital-printing technology, it is possible to reproduce virtually any image on decor paper for a high-resolution result. The image is first scanned and then digitally printed at the factory on a sheet of paper that ends up as a high-pressure laminate. The technology gives designers the opportunity to put original motifs on laminate.

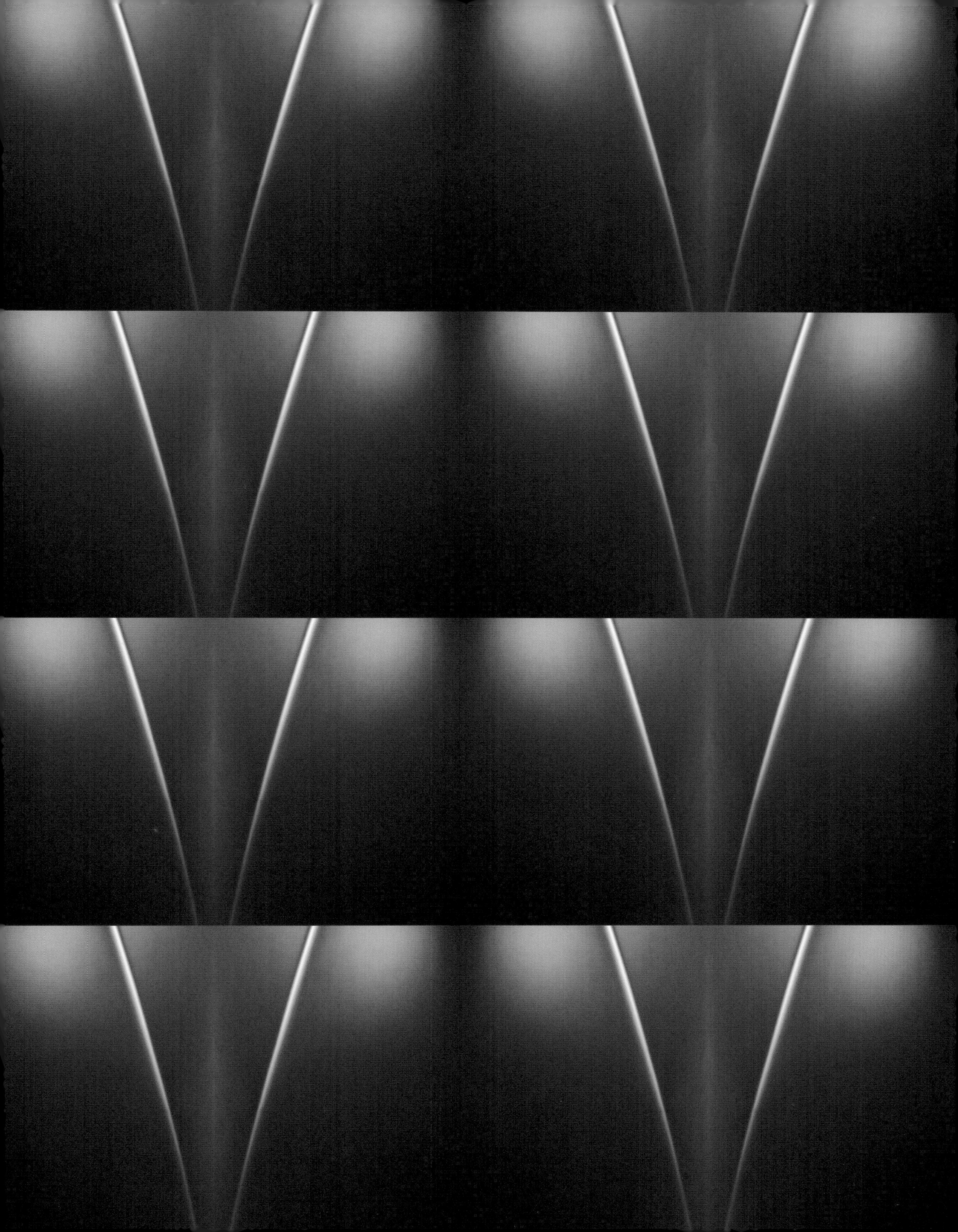

97

ENGINEERED WOOD SURFACE

Composition
Structural composite lumber

Properties
Shrink-resistant, strong, stable, formaldehyde-free, uses green resources, optimal use of trees

Applications
Flooring (planks, parquet weave, tiles), wall panels (laminated), ceiling tiles

Contact
Cozzolino
20 Standish Avenue
West Orange NJ 07052
USA
T +1 973 731 9292
F +1 973 731 0190
mc@cozzolino.com
www.cozzolino.com

Photo
Engineered wood surfaces are stronger, more durable and more multifunctional than non-engineered wood surfaces.

Shrink-resistant, strong and stable are terms seldom applied to solid-wood products. The engineered wood surfaces of Cozzolino's COR (Conserve Our Resources) line, however, are versatile, strong and durable.
COR is made of structurally engineered lumber that utilises op to 76 per cent of the timber harvested for these products (standard wood floors utilise about 40 per cent).
Cozzolino's wood comes from sustainable timber-yield forests with small-diameter trees that are easy to replace with saplings.
The product is available as plank flooring, parquet basket-weave flooring and tiles for floors or walls (in coffee, steel, natural and pickled finishes); as laminated three-ply SCL wall panels; and as ceiling tiles for standard suspension systems.
Certain panels have textured surfaces (examples are diamond- and star-shaped motifs). Products can be custom-manufactured and/or pre-finished; options include acrylic impregnation and surfaces ready for installation. Engineered wood products can be glued or nailed to any prepared surface.

98

INSULATING COATING

Composition
84 per cent solid-latex, high-density material, acrylic polymer binder, blend of pigments

Properties
Insulating, energy-saving, chemical- and corrosion-resistant, eco-friendly, unaffected by UV light, requires little surface preparation, can be tinted any colour, easy to apply, maintains its elasticity, provides condensate control, cost-competitive, reduces use of polyurethane foam, eliminates need for primer, top coating and fibreglass wrap

Applications
Roofs, metal buildings, transportation vehicles, marine projects

Contact
Envirotrol
2594 Flat Shoals Road
Conyers GA 30013
USA
T +1 770 922 4737
F +1 770 922 4279
envirotrol@envirotrol-inc.com
www.envirotrol-inc.com

Photo
The profiled steel roof of this Japanese garage, designed by Klein Dytham architecture, is protected from heat and corrosion by Ceramic Cover insulation coating. Photography by Kozo Takayama.

Marketed as Ceramic Cover, insulating coating is a liquid material whose excellent insulating and corrosion-resistant properties rely on its core substance: amorphous silica, used in the manufacture of ceramics. Encapsulating the ceramic compound is a high-grade acrylic binder, which provides elasticity and good adhesion. The durable material eliminates radiant heat, maintains its tensile strength and elasticity within a wide range of temperatures, and acts as an effective thermal barrier. Environmentally friendly, it contains no carcinogens or volatile organic compounds. The coating requires a single, easy application (no primer, top coating or fibreglass wrap needed) and may be sprayed directly onto hot surfaces without plant shutdown.

99

FELT MATERIALS

Composition
Raw silk, cashmere or wool

Properties
Unwoven structure (end products can vary in structure, thickness, surface texture and density), relies on a matting process suitable for various materials

Applications
Textiles for interior design and apparel

Contact
NTDH
Openhartsteeg 1
NL-1017 BD Amsterdam
The Netherlands
T +31 (0)20 428 4230
F +31 (0)20 620 9673
NTDH@wxs.nl
www.claudyjongstra.com

Photo
Claudy Jongstra creates various types of light, multifaceted felt.

Generally thought of as a rather unyielding material, felt is made with the help of water and friction, a process that usually produces a thick, heavy, matted fabric. After investigating the possibilities of lighter types of felt, designer Claudy Jongstra developed innovative fabrics that bear the label Not Tom Dick & Harry (NTDH). Her fabrics include everything from translucent silks held together by delicate wisps of merino to glamorous reversible organzas made of metallic felt. The materials vary in structure, thickness, surface texture and density. The matting process offers Jongstra an opportunity to combine materials like chiffon and linen with wool and other types of fleece and hair. Because the end result is limited in terms of size, Jongstra is experimenting with ways to create large, seamless pieces of felt. She is working on a joining system that may solve the problem of how to put two or more pieces together invisibly. The connection is strong, and both sides of the material are usable. Applications include carpets, curtains and wall hangings.

00

METAL-BACKED TILES

Composition
Polyester resin or glass, silver or gold foil

Properties
Translucent, rigid, tactile, not cold to the touch, has a three-dimensional effect

Applications
Domestic and contract use

Contact
Natural Tile Company
150 Church Road
Redfield
Bristol BS5 9HN
UK
T +44 (0)117 941 3707
F +44 (0)117 941 3072
sales@naturaltile.co.uk
www.naturaltile.co.uk

Photo
A metal-backed tile featuring crinkled foil comes to life when light hits the surface.

Natural Tile manufactures glass and polyester tiles with a silver and gold backing. Both glass and polyester versions are available in a range of colours and sizes. The metallic foil used for the backing is crinkled to provide depth and vitality to a surface composed of these tiles. All tiles are handmade in batches and therefore subject to variations in colour and size. Among the options available is a tile with a convex surface.

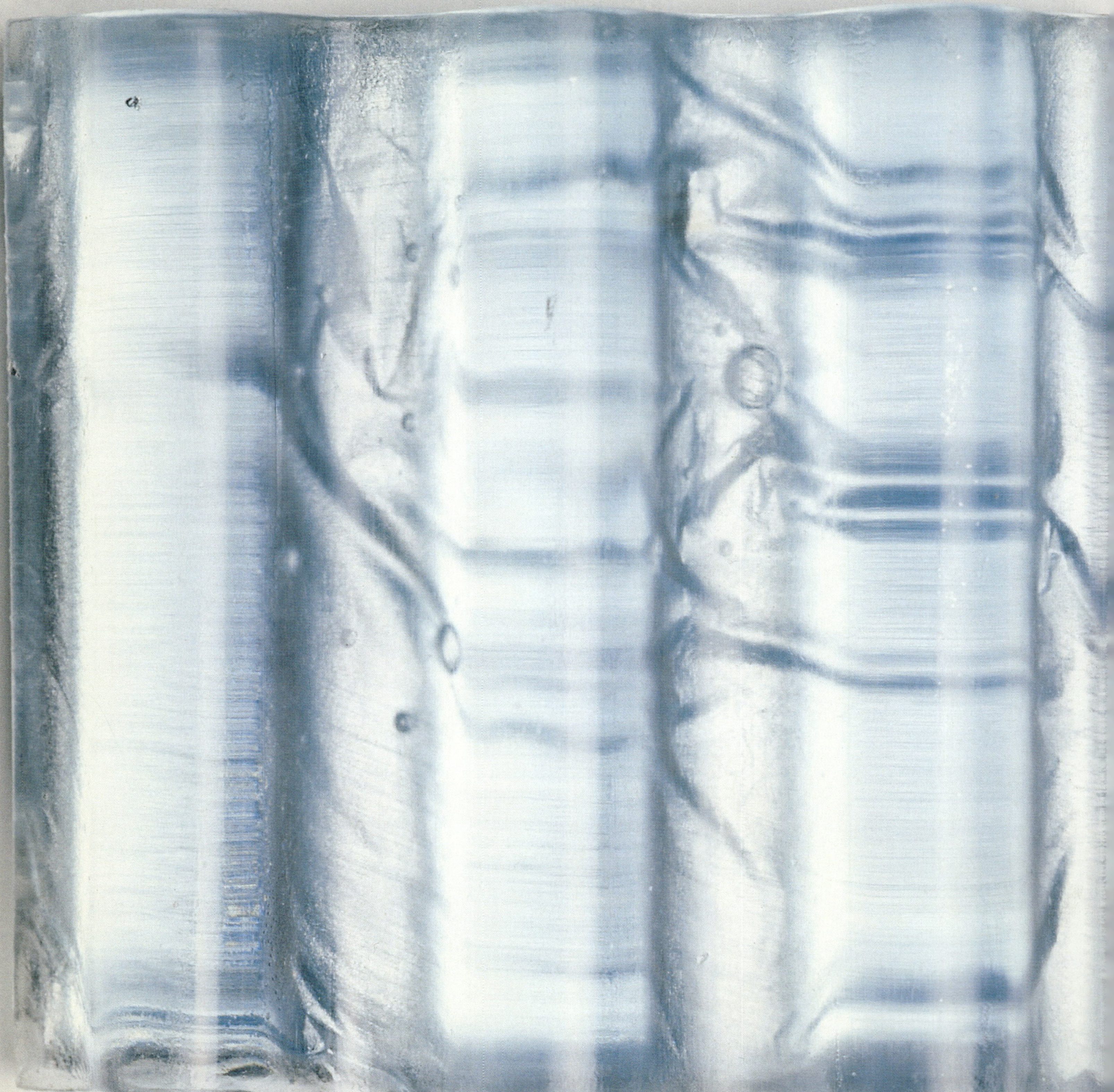

MANUFACTURERS

INDEX

Bonar Floors 53 84
High Holborn Road
Ripley
Derbyshire DE5 3NT
UK
T +44 (0)1773 744 121
F +44 (0)1773 744 142
bonarfloors.uk@lowandbonar.com
www.bonarfloors.com

Braun Wagner 52
Krefelderstrasse 147
D-52070 Aachen
Germany
T +49 (0)2419 973 960
F +49 (0)2419 973 961
info@braunwagner.de
www.braunwagner.de

C

Carnegie RVC 94
110 North Centre Avenue
Rockville Centre NY 11570
USA
T +1 516 678 6770
F +1 516 678 6848
mail@carnegiefabrics.com
www.carnegiefabrics.com
www.xorel.com

Cellbond Composites 58 68
5 Stukeley Business Centre
Blackstone Road
Huntingdon
Cambridgeshire PE29 6EF
UK
T +44 (0)1480 435 302
F +44 (0)1480 432 019
sales@cellbond.com
www.cellbond.co.uk

Clarence House 48
3/10 Chelsea Harbour Design Centre
Chelsea Harbour
London SW10 OXE
UK
T +44 (0)20 7351 1200
F +44 (0)20 7351 6300
sales@clarencehouse.co.uk
www.clarencehouse.com

Comotec 82
Fort des Rousses - BP 42
F-39220 Les Rousses
France
T +33 (0)3 8460 5600
F +33 (0)3 8460 5636
comotec@comotec.com
www.comotec.com

Corus Hylite 71
PO Box 10000
NL-1970 CA IJmuiden
The Netherlands
T +31 (0)251 491 708
F +31 (0)251 471 051
www.corusgroup-hylite.com

Cozzolino 97
20 Standish Avenue
West Orange NJ 07052
USA
T +1 973 731 9292
F +1 973 731 0190
mc@cozzolino.com
www.cozzolino.com

Creative Environments 33
4930 SW 29th Ave.
Dania FL 33312
USA
T +1 954 983 2755
F +1 954 983 2017
ken@illusionflex.com
www.e-iosk.com
www.illusionflex.com

D

Dalsouple 88
PO Box 140
Bridgwater TA5 1 HT
UK
T +44 (0)1984 667 233
F +44 (0)1984 667 366
pr@dalsouple.com
www.dalsouple.com

dcm2 32
Rodenbacher Chaussee 4
Postfach 13 51
D-63403 Hanau-Wolfgang
Germany
T +49 6181 595 308
hans-rolf.goebel@dmc-2.de
www.dcm2.de

Deutsche Gesellschaft für Kunststoff-Recycling 18
Frankfurterstrasse 720-726
D-51145 Cologne
Germany
T +49 (0)2203 931 7743
F +49 (0)2203 931 7828
www.dkr.de

Dimension-Polyant 41
Speefeld 7
D-47906 Kempen
Germany
T +49 (0)2152 891 0
F +49 (0)2152 891 149
info@dimension-polyant.com
www.dimension-polyant.com

DSM High Performance Fibers 51
PO Box 6510
NL-6401 JH Heerlen
The Netherlands
T +31 (0)45 543 6878
F +31 (0)45 543 6800
info.dsmhpf@dsm.com
www.dyneema.com

DSM Somos 78
2 Penn's Way
New Castle DE 19720
USA
T +1 302 328 5435
F +1 302 328 5693
americas@dsmsomos.info
europe@dsmsomos.info
www.dsmsomos.com

DTM 81
26081 Avenue Hall
Valencia CA 91355
USA
T +1 661 295 5600
moreinfo@3dsystems.com
www.dtm-corp.com

DuPont Teijin Films US 45
Barley Mill Plaza, Bldg. 27
Lancaster Pike & Route 141
PO Box 80027
Wilmington DE 19880-0027
USA
T +1 804 530 9339
F +1 804 530 9867
www.duponteijinfilms.com
www.dupont.com/kapton

E

EdiZone LC 39
220 North 1300 West #1
Pleasant Grove UT 84062
USA
T +1 801 785 2767
F +1 801 785 2611
joe@edizone.com
www.edizone.com

ElekSen 06
Pinewood Studios, Pinewood Road
Iver Heath
Buckinghamshire SL0 0NH
UK
T +44 (0)8700 727 272
incoming@eleksen.com
www.eleksen.com

Emdelight 21
Otto-Strasse 7
D-50859 Cologne
Germany
T +49 (0)2234 690 530
F +49 (0)2234 690 528
info@emdelight.com
www.emdelight.com

Envirotrol 98
2594 Flat Shoals Road
Conyers GA 30013
USA
T +1 770 922 4737
F +1 770 922 4279
envirotrol@envirotrol-inc.com
www.envirotrol-inc.com

F

Fielitz 47
Brunnhausgasse 3
D-85049 Ingolstadt
Germany
T +49 (0)841 935 140
F +49 (0)841 935 1413
info@fielitz.de
www.fielitz.de

Flex Products 38
1402 Mariner Way
Santa Rosa CA 95407-7370
USA
T +1 707 525 7007
F +1 707 525 7537
chromaflair@flexprod.com

Fyfe Co. LLC 54
Nancy Ridge Technology Center
6310 Nancy Ridge Drive, Suite 103
San Diego CA 92121
USA
T +1 858 642 0694
F +1 858 642 0947
info@fyfeco.com
www.fyfeco.com

G

G+B pronova 30
Lustheide 85
D-51427 Bergisch-Gladbach
Germany
T +49 (0)2204 204 305
F +49 (0)2204 204 300
contact@gb-pronova.de
www.holopro.com

GDK 43
Metallweberstrasse 46
D-52348 Duren
Germany
info@gdk.de
www.gdk.de

GE Plastics 28
Pittsfield MA
USA
T +1 413 448 7569
www.geplastics.com

H

Heideveld Polyester 75
Europaweg 24
NL-8181 BH Heerde
The Netherlands
T +31 (0)57 869 2058
F +31 (0)57 869 4651
info@heideveld-polyester.nl
www.heideveld-polyester.nl

Henkel Bautechnik 44
PO Box 10 28 52
D-40019 Dusseldorf
Germany
T +49 (0)211 73 790
F +49 (0)211 73 79-290
thomsit@henkel.de
www.henkel.com

Horizon Plastics Company 77
PO Box 474
Cobourg Ontario K9A 4LI
Canada
T +1 905 372 2291
F +1 905 372 9397
horizon@eagle.ca

I

Ineos Acrylics 31
PO Box 34
Darwen
Lancashire BB3 1QB
UK
T +44 (0)125 487 4000
F +44 (0)125 487 3300
perspex_online@ineos-a.com
acrysales@ineos-a.com
www.perspex.co.uk

International Products & Services 14
Via Civesio 6
I-20097 San Donato Milanese (MI)
Italy
T +39 02 527 9641
F +39 02 523 0773
info@ips-srl.it
www.ips-srl.it

J

James Robinson 04
PO Box B3
Hillhouse Lane
Huddersfield HD1 6BU
UK
T +44 (0)1484 320 318
F +44 (0)1484 320 300
uk.sales@james-robinson.ltd.uk
www.james-robinson.ltd.uk

L

Light & Motion Lichttechnik 08
Paulusgasse 13
A-1030 Vienna
Austria
T +43 (0)171 423 26
F +43 (0)171 306 76
info@lightandmotion.at
www.lightandmotion.at

Lintec 29
23-23 Honcho, Itabashi-ku
Tokyo 173-0001
Japan
T +81 (0)3 5248 7711
pub@lintec.co.jp
www.lintec.co.jp

Logitech 06
6505 Kaiser Drive
Fremont CA 94555
USA
T +1 510 795 8500
www.logitech.com

Ludvig Svensson 55
Bangatan 8
SE-511 82 Kinna
Sweden
T +46 (0)320 209 200
F +46 (0)320 211 010
info@ludvigsvensson.com
www.ludvigsvensson.com

M

Madico 29
64 Industrial Parkway
Woburn MA 01801
USA
T +1 781 935 7850
F +1 781 935 6841
amurphy@madico.com
www.madico.com

Makroform 30
Dolivostrasse
D-64293 Darmstadt
Germany
T +49 (0)6151 183 9000
F +49 (0)6151 183 9007
sales@makroform.com
www.makroform.com

Mallinson 02
Unit 5 Gore Cross Business Park
Bridport Dorset DT6 3UX
UK
T +44 (0)1308 427 915
F +44 (0)1308 427 942
info@bendywood.com
www.bendywood.com

Materialise 78 81
Technologielaan 15
B-3001 Leuven
Belgium
T +32 (0)16 396 611
F +32 (0)16 396 600
software@materialise.be
prototype@materialise.be
www.materialise.be

Matsui International Company 86
1501 West 178th Street
Gardena CA 90248
USA
T +1 310 767 7812
F +1 310 767 7836
info@matsui-color.com
www.matsui-color.com

Mazzucchelli 1849 83
Via Santino e Pompeo Mazzucchelli 7
I-21043 Castiglione Olona (VA)
Italy
T +39 03 3182 6111
direzionegenerale@mazzucchelli1849.it
www.mazzucchelli1849.it

MSC Laminates and Composites 36 56
2300 East Pratt Blvd.
Elk Grove Village IL 60007-5995
USA
T +1 847 439 1822
F +1 847 806 2219
www.laminatesandcomposites.com

Muraspec 91
74-78 Wood Lane End
Hemel Hempstead
Hertfordshire HP2 4RF
UK
T +44 (0)870 511 7118
F +44 (0)870 532 9020
customerservices@muraspec.com
www.muraspec.com

N

National Standards Parts 49
4400 Mobile Highway
Pensacola FL 32506
USA
T +1 850 874 6813
F +1 850 456 5376
info@nationalstandardparts.com
www.nationalstandardparts.com

Natural Tile Company 00
150 Church Road
Redfield
Bristol BS5 9HN
UK
T +44 (0)117 941 3707
F +44 (0)117 941 3072
sales@naturaltile.co.uk
www.naturaltile.co.uk

Neon Weka 27
Molenkade 50-51
NL-1115 AC Duivendrecht
The Netherlands
T +31 (0)20 695 1151
F +31 (0)20 695 2241
rob.nolte@neonweka.nl

Noble Fiber Technologies 05
421 South State Street
Clarks Summit PA 18411
T/F +1 570 348 2760
info@noblefiber.com
www.noblefiber.com
info@x-static.com
www.x-static.com

Nuovopovero 75
487/40 Ratchaparob Road
Kweang Makkasan
Khet Ratchatevee 10400 Bangkok
Thailand
T/F +66 (0)2 375 6359
rudolfp@nuovopovero.com
www.nuovopovero.com

P

Panelite 63
600 Broadway, Suite 4c
New York NY 10012
USA
T +1 212 343 0995
F +1 212 343 8187
info@e-panelite.com
www.e-panelite.com

Parabeam 3D Glass Fabrics 42
PO Box 134
NL-5700 AC Helmond
The Netherlands
T +31 (0)492 570 625
F +31 (0)492 570 733
sales@parabeam.nl
www.parabeam3d.com

Pilkington 11
Prescot Road
St. Helens WA10 3TT
UK
T +44 (0)1744 28 882
F +44 (0)1744 692 660
www.pilkington.com
www.activglass.com

The Pilot Ink 03
1F Shizuta Building,
3-7-1 Kotobuki, Taito-Ku
Tokyo
Japan
F +81 (0)3 3844 3052
kawagoe@pilotink.co.jp

Polyline 77
Belgiëlei 4, bus 48
B-2018 Antwerp
Belgium
T +32 (0)32 185 397
F +32 (0)32 185 547
info@polyline.be
www.polyline.be

Project Total Coating 80
Acaciastraat 1
NL-5802 EK Venray
The Netherlands
T +31 (0)478 511 500
F +31 (0)478 510 060
info@ptc.nl
www.ptc.nl

R

RC Tritec 32
Speicherstrasse
CH-9053 Teufen
Switzerland
T +41 (0)71 335 7373
F +41 (0)71 335 7374
sales@rctritec.com
www.rctritec.com

Reflexite Europa 27
Lyngsoe Allé 3
DK-2970 Hoersholm
Denmark
T +45 (0)45 761 122
F +45 (0)45 761 102
europe@reflexite.com
www.reflexite-europe.com

Royal Tichelaar Makkum 85 93 95
PO Box 1
NL-8754 ZN Makkum
The Netherlands
T +31 (0)515 231 341
F +31 (0)515 232 555
info@tichelaar.nl
www.tichelaar.nl

S

Saint-Gobain Glass 09
Les Miroirs, 18, avenue d'Alsace
F-92096 La Défense 3 Cedex
France
T +33 (0)1 4762 3000
R.D@saint-gobain.com
www.saint-gobain.com

Saint-Gobain Glass Nederland 64
PO Box 507
NL-3900 AM Veenendaal
The Netherlands
T +31 (0)318 531 311
F +31 (0)736 413 925
www.saint-gobain.com

Schlegel 87
Rochesterlaan 4
B-8470 Gistel
Belgium
T +32 (0)59 270 300
F +32 (0)59 270 345
isowave@schlegel.be
www.schlegel.be

Schoeller Textil 12 40
Bahnhofstrasse 17
CH-9475 Sevelen
Switzerland
T +41 (0)81 786 0800
F +41 (0)81 786 0810
info@schoeller-textiles.com
www.schoeller-textiles.com

Schott Desag 32
Hattenbergstrasse 10
D-55122 Mainz
Germany
T +49 (0)6131 66-36 62
F +49 (0)6131 66-40 11
klaus.hofmann@schott.com
www.schott.com

Schreinemacher Kunststoffen 31
Gesworenhoekseweg 10
NL-5047 TM Tilburg
The Netherlands
T +31 (0)13 572 9680
F +31 (0)13 572 9689
kunststoffen@schreinemacher.nl
www.schreinemacher.nl

Sekisui Chemical 57
Business, 3-4-7 Toranomon,
Minato-ku
Tokyo 105-8450
Japan
T +81 (0)3 3434 9075
F +81 (0)3 3434 9078
www.sekisui.co.jp

Skyline design 23
1240 North Homan Avenue
Chicago IL 60651
USA
T +1 773 278 4660
F +1 773 278 3548
sales@skydesign.com
www.skydesign.com

Smith & Fong Company 16
375 Oyster Point Blvd. #3
San Francisco CA 94080
USA
T +1 650 872 1184
F +1 650 872 1185
webmaster@durapalm.com
www.durapalm.com

Snowcrash 62
Textilvägen 1
SE-120 30 Stockholm
Sweden
T +46 (0)8 442 9810
F +46 (0)8 442 9811
info@snowcrash.se
www.snowcrash.se

Solutia 34
575 Maryville Centre Drive
St Louis MO 63131
USA
vanceva.solutions@solutia.com
www.vanceva.com

Sommers Plastic Products 19 38
81 Kuller Road
Clifton NJ 07015
USA
T +1 973 777 7888
F +1 973 345 1586
sales@sommers.com
www.sommers.com

Sunovation 07
Vital-Daelen-Strasse
D-63911 Klingenberg-Trennfurt
Germany
T +49 (0)9372 949 109
F +49 (0)9372 949 110
info@sunovation.de
www.sunovation.de

Surfaces+ (Forms+Surfaces) 24 47
6395 Cindy Lane
Carpinteria CA 93013
USA
T +1 877 626 7788
F +1 805 684 8620
marketing@forms-surfaces.com
www.forms-surfaces.com

Swisstex 61
PO Box 9258
Greenville SC 29604-9258
USA
T +1 864 845 7541
F +1 864 845 5699
swissinfo@sprintmail.com
www.swisstex.com

T

Tapetenfabrik Gebr. Rasch 32
Raschplatz 1
49565 Bramsche
Germany
T +49 (0)5461 810
F +49 (0)5461 811 15
info@rasch.de
www.rasch.de

Ten Berge Coating Systems 60
Rijnhavenkade 2
NL-2404 HB Alphen aan den Rijn
The Netherlands
T +31 (0)172 478 888
F +31 (0)172 478 181
info@tenberge.nl
www.tenberge.nl

Textiles y Energia Enertex 46
Mare De Deu Del Pilar St. Andreu De Llavaneres
E-08392 Barcelona
Spain
T +34 (0)6 6978 5112
F +34 (0)93 792 9183
enertex@inicia.es

Treeplast 15
PE Design and Engineering
PO Box 3051
NL-2601 DB Delft
The Netherlands
T +31 (0)15 214 3420
F +31 (0)15 214 3323
info@treeplast.com
www.treeplast.com

Trespa International 90
PO Box 110
NL-6000 AC Weert
The Netherlands
T +31 (0)495 458 850
F +31 (0)495 540 535
infonederland@trespa.com
www.trespa.com

Tricon 45
Hausenerweg 1
D-79111 Freiburg
Germany
T +49 (0)761 490 46-0
F +49 (0)761 490 46-79
scherzinger@tricon-gmbh.de
www.tricon-gmbh.de

HT Troplast 59
Produktbereich Trosifol
Mülheimerstrasse 26
D-53840 Troisdorf
Germany
T +49 (0)2241 853 214
F +49 (0)2241 853 488
www.trosifol.com

U

University of Illinois at Urbana-Champaign 10
Autonomic Healing Research Group
216 Talbot Lab, 104 S. Wright Street
Urbana IL 61801
USA
T +1 217 333 2322
F +1 217 244 5707
www.autonomic.uiuc.edu

W

Well Ausstellungssystem 50
Schwarzer Bär 2
D-30449 Hannover
Germany
T +49 (0)511 92881-10
F +49 (0)511 92881-18
info@well.de
www.well.de

Wogg 70
Im Grund 16
Dättwil
CH-5405 Baden
Switzerland
T +41 (0)56 483 3700
F +41 (0)56 483 3719
info@wogg.ch
www.wogg.ch

Y

Yemm & Hart 18
1417 Madison 308
Marquand MO 63655-9153
USA
T +1 573 783 5434
F +1 573 783 7544
info@yemmhart.com
www.yemmhart.com

DESI
GNE
RS

INDEX

Loods 5 Ontwerpers 20
Generaal Bothastraat 5k
NL-5642 NJ Eindhoven
The Netherlands
T +31 (0)40 281 2000
loods5@chello.nl

Ross Lovegrove 67
21 Powis Mews
London W11 1JN
UK
T +44 (0)20 7229 7104
F +44 (0)20 7229 7032
studiox@compuserve.com

N

NTDH 99
Openhartsteeg 1
NL-1017 BD Amsterdam
The Netherlands
T +31 (0)20 428 4230
F +31 (0)20 620 9673
NTDH@wxs.nl
www.claudyjongstra.com

O

Saar Oosterhof 37
Albrachthof 25
NL-3581 WV Utrecht
The Netherlands
T +31 (0)30 658 6557
F +31 (0)30 658 6556
vormgever@saar.nl
www.saar.nl

Oosterhuis.nl 71
Essenburgsingel 94c
NL-3022 EG Rotterdam
The Netherlands
T +31 (0)10 244 7039
F +31 (0)10 244 7041
oosterhuis@oosterhuis.nl
www.oosterhuis.nl

P

Bill Price 66
12110 Queensbury Lane
Houston TX 77024
USA
T +1 713 743 2400
billpprice@hotmail.com

R

Martín Ruiz de Azúa 45
Aribau 230 8º
E-08006 Barcelona
Spain
T/F +34 (0)93 414 6582
mrazua@teleline.es

MAT ERIA LS

INDEX

T

V

W

GLOSSARY

INDEX

1 centimetre = 0.39 inches
1 metre = 3.28 feet
1 kilometre = 0.62 miles
1 gram = 0.04 ounces
100 grams = 3.53 ounces
1 kilogram = 2.20 pounds (lbs)
1° Celsius = 32° Fahrenheit

A

ABS (acrylonitrile butadiene styrene)
A tough, hard, rigid thermoplastic used especially for making moulded articles. An inexpensive material, ABS provides good chemical and creep resistance and good dimensional stability. It has a tendency to stress crack. Trade names: Cycolac, Cycoloy, Lustran.

ABS/PC (acrylonitrile butadiene styrene/polycarbonate alloy)
A thermoplastic with improved stiffness over conventional high-impact ABS. Easier to process than polycarbonate, it has better notched Izod impact resistance than high-impact ABS (but not as good as that of polycarbonate). Limited resistance to hot water.

acrylic fibre
A thermoplastic fibre made of any of a special group of vinyl compounds, primarily acrylonitrile. Acrylic fibres have low moisture regain, are low in density and can be made into bulky fabrics that wash and dry easily and are dimensionally stable. They are resistant to bleaches, dilute acids and alkalis, as well as to weathering and microbiological attack. Trade names: Orlon, Acrilan.

acrylic resin
A thermoplastic resin used for casting or moulding plastic parts that are exceptionally transparent, tough and resistant to weather and chemicals; or as the main ingredient in coatings, adhesives and caulking compounds. Trade name: Lucite.

aramid
A lightweight polyamide fibre that exhibits high strength and high modulus. Aramid fibres offer good resistance to abrasion, as well as to chemical and thermal degradation. The material can degrade slowly, however, when exposed to ultraviolet light. Trade names: Kevlar, Technora, Twaron.

B

biopolymer
Any of a group of polymers made of fully biodegradable and/or reusable organic substances.

C

CAD (computer-aided design)
The use of computer techniques in designing products, especially involving the use of computer graphics. Designers who employ this method of design use the computer screen as a sophisticated drawing board.

calendering
A method of producing plastic film or sheeting by passing the material between a series of revolving, heated rollers. The technique uses heat and pressure to improve bias stability.

carbon fibre
A black silky thread of pure carbon made by heating and stretching textile fibres and used because of its lightness and strength at high temperatures for reinforcing resins, ceramics and metals. Fibre types range from amorphous carbon to crystalline graphite. The fibres have a high tensile strength (approximately 15 times the strength of construction steel) and high rigidity (up to 3 times the stiffness of steel).

cashmere
A fine soft wool from goats of the Kashmir area that is used to make cloth or knitted material.

casting
A method of shaping a plastic object by pouring the material into a mould and allowing it to harden without the use of pressure.

copolymer
A chemical compound of high molecular weight formed by uniting the molecules of two or more compounds. An example is phenol-formaldehyde.

cotton
Any of various herbaceous plants and shrubs (genus Gossypium) cultivated in warm climates for the fibre surrounding the seeds and the oil within the seeds. The thread or cloth made from this crop is also called cotton.

count
In weaving, count refers to the number of yarns in fill or warp direction. Usually expressed in yarns per inch or centimetre.

CPP (cast polypropylene)
A synthetic thermoplastic material that is 97 per cent polypropylene and 3 per cent polyethylene.

crimp
The natural wave of wool fibres. Woven yarns bend up and down as they pass over and under one another. Crimped yarns are shortened by this bending action and tend to exhibit more stretch.

Cycolac
GE Plastics trade name for ABS/PC.

Cycoloy
GE Plastics trade name for ABS/PC.

D

denier
A unit of weight used to measure the fineness of threads of silk, rayon, nylon and so forth. It is equal to 1 gram per 9000 metres.

E

elastomer
Any material, such as natural or synthetic rubber, that is able to resume its original shape when a deforming force is removed.

epoxy resin
Any of various thermosetting resins (usually amber or brown) capable of forming tight cross-linked polymer structures characterised by toughness, strong adhesion, and high chemical and corrosion resistance. Used especially in surface coatings and adhesives, these resins exhibit low shrinkage during cure, which minimises fabric print-through and internal stress.

F

fibreglass
A reinforced plastic material composed of glass fibres embedded in a resin matrix. Fibreglass is strong, durable and impervious to many caustics and to extreme temperatures. Fibreglass fabrics are widely used for industrial purposes. Trade name: Fiberglas.

flax
Any of a genus (Linum) of plants cultivated for its seeds and the fibres of the stem, which are made into thread and woven into linen fabrics.

formaldehyde
A colourless, poisonous, strong-smelling gas (HCHO) used in solution as a strong disinfectant and preservative, and in the manufacture of synthetic resins and dyes. Primary applications are building materials (adhesive resin used in pressed-wood products) and household products.

H

HPL (high-pressure laminate)
A plastic laminate moulded and cured in the range of pressures from 1200 to 2000 psi (84 to 140 kg per sq cm) used for surfacing countertops and cabinetry. Consists of a high-abrasion top layer, a decorative sheet and a sheet of phenolic-resin-treated kraft.

I

Inconel
Trade name of a nickel-based alloy used in industrial applications requiring a strong material that resists oxidation at high temperatures.

injection moulding
A method of forming a thermoplastic, thermoset, metal or ceramic material by rendering it fluid in a heating chamber and then forcing it under high pressure into a closed mould.

ITO (indium tin oxide)
Indium tin oxide is a metallic coating material that blocks up to 90 per cent of light transmission in the near infrared. It can be vacuum deposited on glass and plastic to provide an effective antistatic shield.

K

Kapton
DuPont trade name for polyimide film.

Kevlar
DuPont trade name for aramid.

L

laminate
A product made by uniting two or more layers of material by an adhesive or other means. Examples are plywood and plastic laminate

latex
A whitish milky fluid produced by many plants. Latex from the rubber tree (Hevea brasiliensis) is used in the manufacture of rubber. The latex used in paints and adhesives is a water emulsion of synthetic rubber or plastic globules obtained by polymerisation.

LCD (liquid-crystal display)
A flat-screen display in which an array of liquid-crystal elements can be selectively activated to generate an image, an electric field applied to each element altering its optical properties.

LED (light-emitting diode)
A semiconductor diode that emits light when voltage is applied. Applications include lamps, alphanumeric displays (digital watches), measuring instruments, microcomputers and lasers.

M

melamine
A colourless, crystaline compound used in making synthetic thermosetting resins. These amino resins, which are stable to heat and light, are formed by the interaction of melamine and formaldehyde. They are used to make moulded products, adhesives and surface coatings. Melamine products are highly resistant to heat and physical or chemical degradation; they enhance the hardness, gloss and scratch-resistance of surfaces. Certain types have flame-retardant and/or moisture-resistant properties.

merino
The long fine wool of the merino sheep. The soft, lustrous yarn made from this wool is available in grades of 23 microns or finer. The fibres, which are as fine as cashmere, are highly crimped for strength and elasticity.

Monel metal
Trade name of a silvery, corrosion-resistant alloy consisting of nickel (67 per cent), copper (28 per cent), and smaller quantities of such metals as iron, manganese and aluminium.

monofilament
Synthetic thread or yarn composed of a single strand rather than twisted fibres.

N

nylon (polyamide)
A class of synthetic polyamide materials made by copolymerising dicarboxylic acids with diamines. These inexpensive, lightweight thermoplastics are strong and elastic; they can be extruded into filaments, fibres, sheets and moulded objects. Applications include bearings, blow mouldings and fabric.
A disadvantage is poor dimensional stability caused by water absorption.

O

OPP (oriented polypropylene)
A packaging material derived from melting and orienting (stretching) polypropylene. OPP film protects surfaces from moisture, grease and oxygen. It is excellent for high-quality printing.

organza
A thin, stiff, translucent fabric made of materials such as silk, cotton, rayon and nylon.

P

PA (polyamide)
See nylon.

PCM (phase change materials)
Collective term for materials capable of changing their physical state within a given range of temperatures: from solid to liquid and vice versa.

PE (polyethylene or polythene)
A tough, light, flexible thermoplastic material made of ethylene. The properties of this synthetic resin depend on the molecular weight of the polymer used. The world's most popular plastic, PE is used for packaging, toys, insulation, textiles, metal coatings, damp-proofing – even bulletproof vests. The versatility of the material is complemented by its simple structure, the most uncomplicated of all commercial polymers.

PET (polyethylene terephthalate)
A synthetic resin made by copolymerising ethylene glycol and terephthalic acid. Chief applications are bottles and fibres.

PETG (polyethylene terephthalate glycolate)
Also known as glycolised polyester, PETG is an amorphous, highly impact-resistant copolyester that does not crystallise. Glycolate minimises brittleness and increases durability. Properties include clarity and thermoformability.

phenolic resin (phenoplast)
Any of a class of hard, heat-resistant thermosetting resins formed by the condensation of phenol with formaldehyde. Used for moulded products, adhesives and surface coatings such as paints. This dense material is made by applying heat and pressure to layers of paper or glass cloth impregnated with synthetic resin. The result is a chemical reaction (polymerisation), which transforms the layers into a high-pressure thermosetting industrial laminated plastic. Trade name: Bakelite.

photopolymer
A light-sensitive polymeric material, especially one used in printing plates or microfilms.

photovoltaic
Of, concerned with, or generating an electromotive force at the junction of two substances exposed to visible or other radiation.

piezoelectric
Able to convert mechanical signals (such as sound waves) into electrical signals, and vice versa. Piezoelectric crystals are used in products such as microphones and earphones; they can also generate a spark for lighting gas appliances.

plastic laminate
A hard surfacing material consisting of superimposed layers of paper impregnated with melamine and phenolic resins, fused together under heat and pressure.

PMMA (polymethyl-methacrylate)
A clear vinyl polymer. This acrylic resin is used as a shatterproof replacement for glass. Trade names: Plexiglas, Lucite.

Polyamide
See nylon.

polycarbonate
A tough, transparent, nontoxic thermoplastic characterised by high-impact strength, remarkable thermal resistance and good electrical properties. Polycarbonate resins are used in moulding materials and laminates: examples are lighting fixtures, safety glazing and hardware. Trade name: Lexan (a product used for shatterproof windows and decorative resins).

polyester
Any of a large group of thermosetting resins used in the manufacture of plastics, textile fibres and adhesives. These polymers are characterised by extremely long molecules, each of which is several thousand atoms long; a polyester fibre resembles a tiny rope made of microscopic spaghetti. Trade names: Dacron (polyester fibre), Mylar (polyester film).

polymer
A compound of high molecular weight formed by polymerisation and consisting essentially of repeating structural units.

polymerisation
A chemical reaction in which the molecules of a monomer combine to form larger molecules that contain repeating structural units of the original molecules.

polyolefin
Any of a group of plastics that are polymers of various alkenes. (Alkenes are also known as olefins or olefines.) The most important polyolefins are polyethylene and polypropylene.

polypropylene
A tough, flexible thermoplastic that is resistant to heat and chemicals. The material is made by polymerising propylene. Applications include moulded articles, laminates, bottles, pipes, electrical insulation, films, and fibres for ropes, bristles, upholstery and carpets.

polyurethane
Any of various thermoplastic or thermosetting resins used in flexible and rigid foams, elastomers, and resins for sealants, adhesives and coatings. The material is made by copolymerising an isocyanate and a polyhydric alcohol. Flexible polyurethane rubber is used in furniture and automobile cushions, mattresses, and carpet backings. Rigid polyurethane foam is used for packing, as well as for the thermal insulation of refrigerators, trucks and buildings.

polyvinyl resin
Any of a class of thermoplastic resins that are made by polymerising or copolymerising a vinyl compound. The commonest type is PVC.

prepegs
Pre-compressed fibre mats made of softwood fibres and thermosetting phenolic resin in a dry-forming process. Application: durable wall covering.

PS (polystyrene)
A hard, tough, stable thermoplastic obtained by polymerising styrene. PS is easily coloured and moulded, expanded, or rolled into sheeting. This synthetic resin is used as a lightweight, rigid foam (expanded polystyrene) for insulating and packing, and as a glasslike material in light fittings and water tanks. Other applications are films and chemical apparatus.

PTFE (polytetrafluoroethylene)
A white, thermoplastic material with a waxy texture, made by polymerising tetrafluoroethylene. It is nonflammable, resists chemical action and radiation, and has a high electrical resistance and an extremely low coefficient of friction. It is used for making gaskets, hoses, insulators, bearings, and for coating metal surfaces in chemical plants and in nonstick cooking vessels. Trade name: Teflon (made by DuPont).

PVB (polyvinyl butyral)
A thermoplastic resin used chiefly as the interlayer of laminated safety glass.

PVC (polyvinyl chloride)
A white, water-insoluble, synthetic thermo-plastic material made by polymerising vinyl chloride. Properties depend on the added plasticiser. PVC is widely used in the manufacture of floor coverings, insulation and piping.
Other applications are shoes, garments and moulded articles.

PZT (lead zirconate titanate)
One of a class of piezoelectric materials.

R

resin
Any of numerous solid or semisolid organic substances prepared by polymerisation and used with fillers, stabilisers and other components to form plastic.

rubber
A material made by chemically treating and toughening natural rubber, valued for its elasticity, nonconduction of electricity, and resistance to shock and moisture.

S

SCL
Abbreviation for structural composite lumber.

silicone rubber
A rubber made from silicone elastomers and noted for its retention of flexibility, resilience and tensile strength over a wide temperature range.

silk
A fine, strong, soft lustrous fibre produced by silkworms in making cocoons. An important component is sericin, a resinous, amorphous substance that bonds the two gossamer filaments of raw silk. Thread and fabric made from this material are also called silk.

Spectra
Trade name of a polyethylene with an ultra-high molecular weight and outstanding properties: low specific gravity, high specific strength, low moisture sensitivity, excellent chemical resistance, high impact resistance, high specific modulus, high abrasion resistance and excellent electrical properties. Spectra is ten times stronger than steel. So tough that it will not accept dye, Spectra fibre is available only in white.

T

Technora
Trade name of a para-aramid fibre made of copolymers. Properties are high tensile strength, high modulus and excellent resistance to heat and chemicals, especially acids and alkalis. Technora, which has countless industrial applications, is used to reinforce rubber, cement and plastic.

thermoforming
A method of shaping a thermoplastic sheet by heating and forcing it against the contours of a mould with compressed air.

thermoplastic
A plastic capable of softening or fusing when heated without a change in any inherent properties, and of hardening again when cooled.

thermosetting plastic
A plastic that becomes permanently rigid when heated and cannot be softened again.
(Also called thermoset.)

titanium
A silvery or dark grey, lustrous, metallic element (symbol: Ti) found in rutile and other minerals and used as a cleaning and deoxidising agent in molten steel, and in the manufacture of aircraft, satellites and chemical equipment. It has the highest strength-to-weight ratio of any known element. Titanium is impervious to most chemicals and extremely resistant to corrosion.

Twaron
Akzo Nobel trade name for aramid.

twine
Strong thread, string or cord of two or more strands twisted together. Cotton and hemp are two materials commonly used to make twine.

V

Vectran
High-performance thermoplastic multifilament yarn spun from Vectra liquid crystal polymer (LCP), a Celanese product. It is a very strong fibre with minimal stretch and no propensity to creep. Excellent abrasion resistance combined with good fatigue strength prevents sudden breakage. Poor resistance to UV light indicates the need for a covering.

vinyl
Any vinyl polymer, resin or plastic, especially PVC.

vinylester resin
Vinylester resins are similar in their molecular structure to polyesters, but differ primarily in the location of their reactive sites, these being positioned only at the ends of the molecular chains. As the whole length of the molecular chain is available to absorb shock loadings, vinylester resins are tougher and more resilient than polyesters. The vinylester molecule also features fewer ester groups. These ester groups are susceptible to water degradation by hydrolysis, which means that vinylesters are more resistant to water and certain chemicals than their polyester counterparts. Applications include pipelines and chemical storage tanks.

viscose
An amber-coloured, viscous solution made by treating cellulose with sodium hydroxide and carbon disulphide. It is used to make rayon thread and fabrics, and cellophane. Viscose rayon has a shinier finish and holds dye better than cotton does.

W

warp
The yarns arranged lengthways on a loom, forming the threads through which the weft yarns are woven.

weft
The yarn woven across the width of the fabric through the lengthways warp yarn.

wool
Yarn spun from the fleece of sheep (primarily), goats or llamas.

X

X-Ply
Manufactured by Dimension Polyant, X-Ply is the trade name of a fabric with off-the-warp support. The fabric is produced by inserting continuous yarns at various angels of the warp in an 'X' pattern.

Y

yarn
A continuous twisted strand of natural or synthetic fibres – such as wool, silk, flax, cotton, nylon or glass – used for weaving, knitting or making thread.

ABOUT THE AUTOR

Edwin van Onna, Dutch publicist and art historian, was a former faculty member of the Department of Visual Arts and Design at the Utrecht Academy of Art. Van Onna regularly writes about design for a number of publications, including *Frame*.

COLOPHON

Material World
Innovative Structures and Finishes
for Interiors

Publishers
Frame Publishers
www.framemag.com
Birkhäuser — Publishers for Architecture
www.birkhauser.ch

Compiled and written by
Edwin van Onna

Introduction by
Ed van Hinte

Graphic design
De Designpolitie
www.designpolitie.nl

Copy editing
Donna de Vries-Hermansader

Translation
InOtherWords (Donna de Vries-Hermansader)

Photography
All photos are made by Daniël Nicolas,
unless otherwise indicated

Colour reproduction
Graphic Link

Printing
Hoonte Bosch & Keuning

Distribution
Benelux, China, Japan, Korea
and Taiwan
ISBN 90-806445-6-0
Frame Publishers
Lijnbaansgracht 87
NL-1015 GZ Amsterdam
The Netherlands
www.framemag.com

All other countries
ISBN 3-7643-6745-8
Birkhäuser — Publishers for Architecture
P.O. Box 133
CH-4010 Basel
Switzerland
Member of the BertelsmannSpringer
Publishing Group
www.birkhauser.ch

A CIP catalogue record for this book is available
from the Library of Congress, Washington D.C.,
USA

Deutsche Bibliothek Cataloging-in-Publication
Data
Material world - innovative structures and
finishes for interiors /
[comp. and written by Edwin van Onna. Transl.
Donna de Vries-Hermansader]. -
Basel ; Boston ; Berlin : Birkhäuser; Amsterdam
: Frame Publ., 2003
ISBN 3-7643-6745-8
ISBN 90-806445-6-0

Printed on acid-free paper produced from
chlorine-free pulp. TCF∞
Printed in the Netherlands
987654321

MAT
ERIA
LWO
RLD

INNO
VATI
VES
TRU
CTU
RES